Kong: Becoming a King of API Gateways

By Alex Kovalevych, Robert Buchanan, Daniel Lee, Chelsy Mooy, Xavier Bruhiere, and Jose Ramon Huerga

Kong: Becoming a King of API Gateways

ISBN: 9781939902566

Published by: Bleeding Edge Press, Santa Rosa, CA 95404

Title: Kong: Becoming a King of API Gateways

Authors: Alex Kovalevych, Robert Buchanan, Daniel Lee, Chelsy Mooy, Xavier Bruhiere, and Jose Ramon Huerga

Acquisitions Editor: Christina Rudloff

Editor: Troy Mott

Website: bleedingedgepress.com

Table of Contents

Preface

Who is this book for?

This book is useful for IT architects, DevOps engineers, CTOs and security experts willing to understand how to use Kong to create and expose APIs.

Even if you are not already familiar with Kong, it will only take a few minutes to create your first API.

What do you need to know prior to reading?

You don't need to know Kong to read this book! You only need to have a basic understanding of REST, JSON and HTTP, but you don't need an in-depth knowledge because Kong's mission is to provide easy API publishing.

You will also need a modern browser: Google Chrome, Mozilla Firefox, Microsoft Edge or Apple Safari.

The online example

All of the code for the sample project in this book can be found at:

https://github.com/backstopmedia/kong-book-example

What will this book provide?

By the end of this book, you will understand how to:

- Use an API gateway to simplify and improve the security of your microservices architecture
- Write Kong plugins with Lua
- Deploy Kong and Cassandra in a multi-region environment

- Use load balancing features.

Book co-authors and contributors

Alex Kovalevych is an experienced web developer from Kyiv, Ukraine. Having degrees in computer science and finance, he is a polyglot web developer, constantly learning and using cutting edge technologies. He has been working on different worldwide projects in gaming and health fields.

Chelsy Mooy has been handling multiple SaaS for Finance projects as a CTO and Co-Founder of PT Thunderlabs Indonesia. She believes that well-constructed technology is a powerful "bunshin no jutsu." She lives in Malang, Indonesia with "the dog" and wears a skirt on Sunday.

Daniel Lee is a skilled engineer and is enthusiastic about tech. He really loves data science, cloud engineering, and service development. He was a former chief developer at the web community Yourssu, and now he is running a legal tech startup, Dbrain Science, in South Korea.

Robert Buchanan is a passionate, forever learning software craftsman that picks the right tool for the right job. He is a polyglot engineer who has been in all aspects of the cycle as a UI developer, service developer, cloud engineer and performance analyst. He lives with his wife and kid in Northern Kentucky, United States.

Xavier Bruhiere is a senior data engineer growing the Kpler team in Singapore. He has been crunching data since founding his own quantitative investment company and through startups in Paris. He loves to collaborate with smart people, visiting new countries and eating Italian delights.

Jose Ramon Huerga Ayuso is an API Management and Microservices expert. During the 80s he was a teenage programmer and later in the 90s he earned a degree in computer science. He has been working in multiple fields, including SOA, QA, ECM, and CRM. He lives with his wife and two kids in Madrid, Spain.

Technical Reviewers

We would like to the thank the following technical reviewers for their early feedback and generous, careful critiques: Nicolas Huray and Michallis Pashidis. Thanks also to Eber Herrera, Panagis Tselentis, and Damian Czaja.

Microservices architecture 1

Have you ever thought about marching bands? There are groups of brass players, woodwind players, percussion players, and color guards that join together and play their role without being dependent on each other. Any individual player can be replaced or upgraded without disrupting the entire instrumental section.

Microservices are like this: any one part can be replaced without breaking down the entire system.

Let's take a cinema system as an example. You can always check which movies are showing. You can also check if the movies have been well reviewed, you can reserve a ticket (or two), and you can be notified when new movies are showing (of course, in your favorite genre). As the requirements grow, you can add more features like blacklisting users, or embedding a payment gateway that helps customers when paying for tickets. But in this scenario you have to test the whole system to make sure that changes don't affect other parts of the system, and you need to take the system offline when making upgrades. With microservices, however, you don't need to test the entire system and you don't need to take it offline.

Monolith's most popular patterns in view of Microservices

There are several design patterns used in a monolith architecture to scale up the system. The most popular patterns are three-tier architectures and MVC. In microservices both patterns are used in order to build a single service or to compose services.

Three-tier architecture

Three-tier architecture separates development based on three layers:

1. Data Access Layer (DAL) is a layer where we define our entities and their relationships. This is the core of the whole system. Because of the `core` word, this is the last layer that should be changed or modified.
2. Business Logic Layer (BLL) is where we put business policies and workflows. It controls whole business events and their responses. Because policies and workflows change from time to time, this layer should dynamically change.
3. Presentation Layer (UIL) is the upper layer that is seen and interacts with the end user of an app. This layer is dependent on devices, whether they are desktop apps, web apps, or mobile apps.

Three-tier architecture is used to better maintain processes. This architecture is commonly modified and used in microservices. For example, you can put a data access layer and business logic layer in a service level, and the presentation layer in the client level. In the other example, implementing three tiers in level of services, clients only need to fetch requests to display views. This second option is not frequently used.

MVC architecture

Model-View-Controller (MVC) architecture is widely used in popular web-based frameworks like Ruby on Rails and Laravel. Model represents the Data Access Layer and the Business Logic Layer, while View and Controller represent the Presentation Layer. Just like with three tiers architecture, the MVC architecture is often modified and used in microservices.

Microservices answer

Using microservices is not only about chunking the monolith into pieces, because the whole mindset is different. It is much more than just separating layers. Some microservices characteristics may help explain what microservices can and should be.

Bounded Context

Before stepping out into the microservices world, the very first thing to know is bounded context, which allows you to focus on the core context and its logic. It is quite similar to the domain context in the domain design driven approach. Looking back at our example cinema system, you can break the system down into smaller contexts:

1. Movie service provides detailed information about movies like: movie title, ratings, casts, etc.
2. Show Time Service is responsible for handling movie schedules in specific theaters and how much it costs.
3. Booking Service allows customers to book which movie they'd like to watch and when, and reserve their seat for a certain showtime.
4. Users Service defines information about users. For example, an employee or a customer, name, email, password, etc.

When the requirements grow, like giving recommendations for new releases to our customers, or blacklisting a customer who was caught recording the movie with his/her phone, or even embedding a system with a payment gateway like PayPal, you can just add more services without worrying that it will cause problems with other services.

Small in size

How small is micro in microservices?

Doing microservices is an art, so there are no specific rules about how it is done. But it should be enough to handle the context. The context can be composed of a verb, noun, or even a hybrid of a verb-noun. The small size makes it easier to be replaced or upgraded.

Various platforms

Microservices allow you to deploy services in various platforms. You can deploy a movie service in Python using MongoDB, for example, and deploy a showtime service using PHP and MySql.

Y axis scaling

Microservices are not running multiple-identical copies of an application, instead they split an application into multiple-different services. A common scaling mode is a 3 * 3 dimensional cube, which consists of 18 similar little cubes. Microservices are more like a lego house, which is built upon different types of 3D geometric shapes, like rectangulars or triangular prisms where each prism is responsible for one context.

Ideal environment of microservices

Microservices are not an answer to every problem. There are requirements that allow microservices to run in an ideal environment:

1. Big Systems: Microservices were created to solve problems for `big` systems. That's why a microservices' architecture, pattern, and technology make sense to cases like Netflix or Spotify. Microservices is prepared to solve problems like crowded traffic, ever-changing requirements, technologies, patterns, and business, along with how to handle different flows of a big system and to be fast and light at the same time. The word `big` has no particular measurement, but you can say it should be `big` enough to break down into contexts.
2. Goal Oriented: Since there is a need for scaling up, services are goal oriented. If a service is designed to focus on one thing, it is then easier to upgrade or even replace the service without breaking the flow, which is the DNA of microservices.
3. Replaceability: As written above, microservices aim to be replaced or upgraded without interrupting the flow. It's driving the development process to replace a service instead of maintaining a service. As you know, maintaining a service is the most costly in the development phase.

Communicating with the world

Let's say you have services built independently, but you need to orchestrate these various platforms of services into a harmony to run a workflow or a business scenario. What is the best way to do this?

Does a different service mean a different engine?

Microservices allow you to put a service in whenever you want to, anywhere. As for the previous case, there is an issue about whether an endpoint should be able to handle multiple requests from various frontend engines. Instead of an obligation to put services in a different engine, we need to actually put it in a different engine.

Let's say we need to build multiple frontend interfaces for our cinema system:

1. Responsive web app for browsers
2. Native Android app

Both of these frontend interfaces need different data content. For example, in an Android app you need to display a customer's name, a movie showtime list that contains information like title, and show time and price. The web app needs to display more details like a movies' short description, ratings, and main casts. The questions are:

1. Should our web app know all of the addresses of our services? And should it make a request for each piece of information as needed?
2. Is it okay to let our bare services be exposed to all frontend interfaces?
3. Should the Android app fetch all data, which means the consumption of more bandwidth, when only some data is needed?

Using an API gateway

Implementing an API Gateway as an interface to our services will help solve the problems described in the previous section.

1. We can wrap data from various services into one response in one request, and at the same time protect our services address from the 'outside world.' For example, instead of calling `http://users.mycinemas.com/details/me` and `http://showtime.mycinemas.com/lists`, we can just call `http://kongcinemas.com/movies/lists`.

The scenario of a calling service is a benefit for us. If we're going to change our services address, only one place needs to be changed (you don't have to change all interface request addresses).

Instead of making two connections, frontend apps make only one connection through the API Gateway in order to fetch data that is needed by a single app. Besides, all of the exposed addresses are always API Gateway addresses.

1. An API Gateway also works as an authentication and authorization engine for frontend interfaces, and it can log all of their requests. As for our case, the API Gateway is able to make differences between requests from Android apps or web apps. Feel free to visit Chapter 9 to learn more about this.
2. An API Gateway allows you to transform or limit data that you need. This then saves bandwidth, prevents malicious action and fake calls, and more.

API Gateway variation

There are many ways of using an API Gateway. You can have one API Gateway for one client or one API Gateway for multiple clients.

A pattern called Backends For Frontends (BFF) has two clients: responsive web apps and native Android apps. It also has two different API gateways. Each of those Gateways provide services for each client. So, when is the right time to use BFF or a single API Gateway?

Let's say that a responsive web app was built by a web developer team, and a native Android app was built by an Android developer team. Separate teams working on different interfaces might cause bottlenecks in the development process. On the other hand, different interfaces mean different requirements due to device performance. This might cause conflicts while updating requirements, since an API Gateway must be able to handle different requirements in one way. This means that more effort is required to deploy an API Gateway than what every client needs. Changes in backend services needs to be validated by both interface teams before they are implemented.

Let's look again at our cinema system. The native Android app needs more interactive features. In order to fulfill that purpose, our API Gateway needs have a specific-purpose backend. That's the ideal time to implement a Backends For Frontends pattern.

Multiple servers for one services

Another usage of the API Gateway is load balancing, which efficiently distributes network traffic across services, making it possible to run multiple servers of services in concurrent time. Let's say we have three requests for showtime service, and an API Gateway that helps us assign which request should be handle by which services. This means that all requests can get a responses in almost the same time, with no need to wait.

Summary

You should now have a good understanding of microservices, and in the next chapter we will look in more detail at API Gateways and Kong.

2 API Gateway - A rapidly changing landscape

When the Internet started there was only the concept of an HTTP Server that would serve up static web pages. That quickly grew into having application servers that served up web applications or servlets using HTTP Servers as reverse proxies to the applications. While these applications were great for the time, they became too large to allow integrations in a Service Oriented Architecture (SOA) with other applications/services, which lead to the creation of an Enterprise Service Bus (ESB).

All of the code for the sample project in this book can be found **here**.

What is an ESB?

An ESB implements a communication system between mutually interacting software applications in SOA. As an architecture, an ESB can be thought of as a central platform for integrating applications in an enterprise. It can also be thought of as an architecture that allows communication via a common communication bus that consists of a variety of point-to-point connections between providers and users of services.

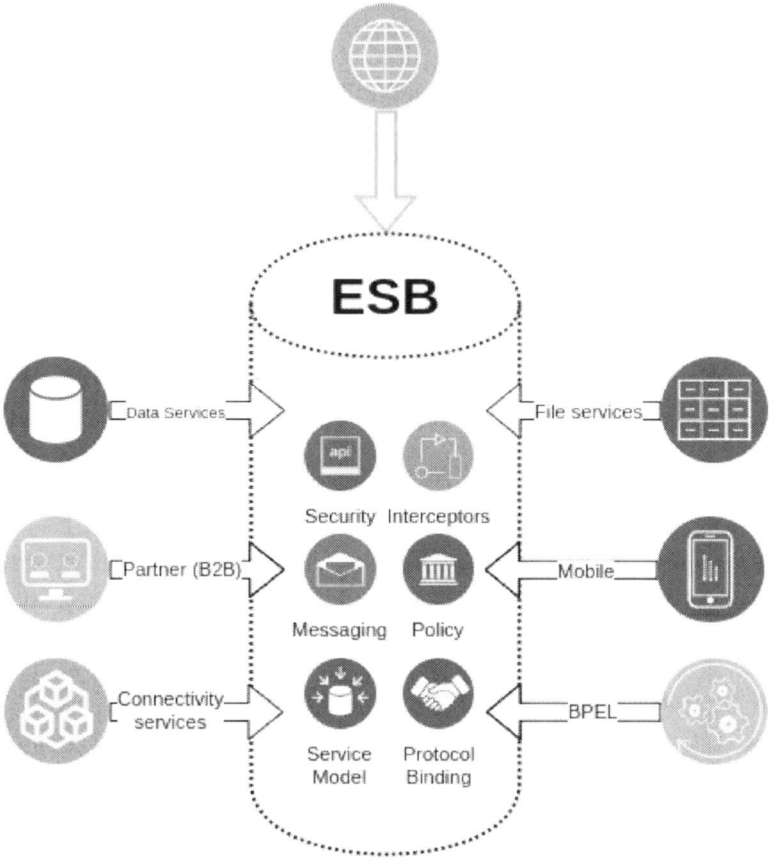

An ESB promotes agility and flexibility with regard to high-level protocol communication (XML to JSON, and vice versa) between applications. The main goal of this high-level protocol communication is Enterprise Application Integration (EAI) of complex service or application landscapes in a maintainable manner. Some of its primary duties of an ESB are to route messages between services, monitor and control routing messages between services, control the versioning of services, and provide commodity services like data transformation and security. An ESB is generally used to facilitate the internal communication between services, but isn't limited to this use case.

What is an API Gateway?

API Gateways are essentially glorified reverse proxies that offer more customizations and flexibility to reverse proxies. An API Gateway acts as an API frontend that orchestrates API Requests, enforces traffic policies (i.e. throttling, caching), security policies (i.e. authorization, authentication), gathers analytics on traffic, and orchestrates transformation engines for modifying requests/responses on the fly. An API Gateway is generally seen as the entry point for communication between the external requests and the internal services, hence its name. Using an API Gateway internally, however, can facilitate great rewards in terms of the standardization of policies.

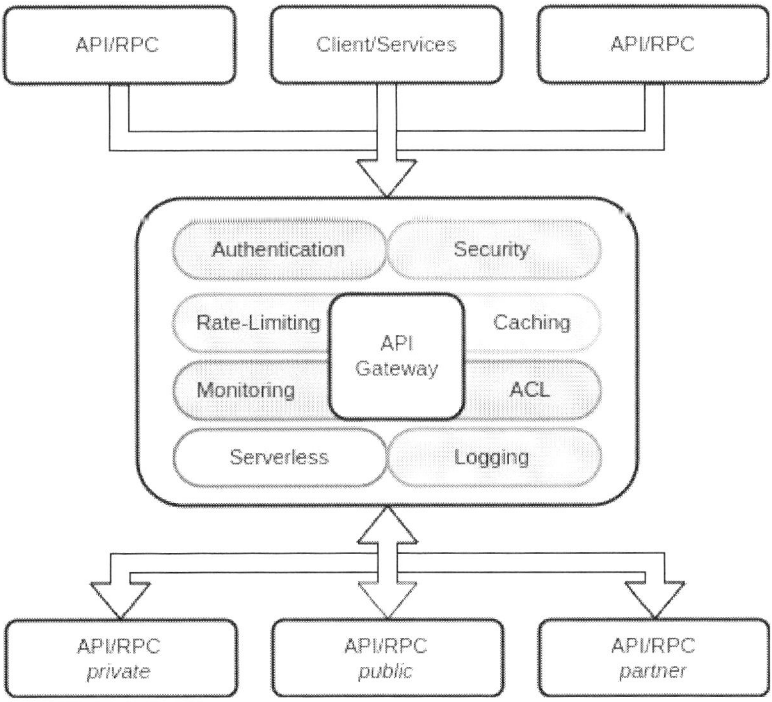

Is an API Gateway a new ESB?

Are API Gateways a re-invention of the ESB? Yes and no. Although an API Gateway may provide a lot of the same functionality (security, data transformation, routing), it does it in an orchestrated way instead of a point-to-point or broadcast way. An API Gateway and ESB can live side-by-side because their primary duties overlap their intended purposes and they are separated by concerns of internal and external communication.

The equivalent of an ESB to animals is the nervous system combined with the circulatory system. When an organ needs to communicate with another specific organ, it uses the nervous system to send a point-to-point message. When an organ needs to broadcast a message to other organs that might be interested, it releases a hormone into the bloodstream to send a multicast message. When a message comes into the brain from anywhere in the body, the brain tells the body how to react. For example, if you accidentally touch a hot stove, the nerves in your skin shoot a message of pain to your brain. The brain then sends a message back telling the muscles in your hand to pull away. The API Gateway is equivalent to the brain in the way that it orchestrates interaction.

Although the API Gateway can be thought of as a brain, it doesn't mean that it doesn't need or isn't enhanced by the nervous system. So, when looking at the current landscape, API Gateways are not a new ESB, but an enhancement of the original concept of an ESB.

API Gateway present

Back in time there were Neanderthals who discovered fire, and from fire they discovered cooking, and from cooking they were able to live longer. As they lived longer they started to want more than just a cave and they started building. First we had houses (HTTP Servers), then tribes (Reverse Proxies), then villages (ESB), and then we built towns. A town is small enough that everyone knows what is going on and can help out while being big enough that there is a need for a centralized way to manage the developments happening in the town. Most companies are the size of towns, and they have a lot of domain knowledge and offerings that a centralized API Gateway can fulfill their needs with, and they won't need to be concerned with what is happening in the other towns.

In the present landscape there are a lot of well established offerings for API Gateways such as Kong, APIGEE, KrakenD, Tyk.io and IBM API Connect (previously Strongloop). Each one of these offerings has their advantages and disadvantages, from price, maintainability, scalability and customization.

API Gateway future

Although a lot of companies enjoy their peaceful town there are companies that are evolving into cities. While evolving from a town to a city the amount of buildings grows exponentially and planning the city becomes too big of a job for a single centralized contact, so the mayor has to employ a team to handle the planning.

With the orchestration of services in the microservice architectures becoming increasingly difficult, new developments into the API Gateway space have emerged to leverage other recent developments in tech.

Serverless

Functions as a Service (FaaS) (i.e. Amazon's Lambda, OpenWhisk) were created not too long ago but have most recently become stable and a selling point to leverage as an API Gateway. When you breakdown an API Gateway it is really a stack of functions that chain off each other to fulfill a request. Thinking about an API Gateway in this fashion led to the use of FaaS platforms to facilitate API Gateway functions. There are several out there but one in particular that has been used heavily is the **Serverless framework**. This has been proven to be a good use case for simple API gateways, especially if you are already using FaaS technology for other business needs. It does mean that every aspect of your API Gateway needs must be coded, generally by your company. With Serverless the idea is that you do not have to run your own infrastructure. This can be a selling point to some, but it also means you are at the mercy of your providers network, policies, and operational capabilities. Using FaaS from a big provider like Google/AWS is ideal, but not every company is comfortable with having other people host their data, especially since any data breaches are a PR nightmare causing the demise of a company.

Service Meshes

As containerization became popular for the purpose of removing the overhead of running a full operating system just to host an application, it quickly became abused and now everything is its own container. This problem of every app as its own container spawned companies to have several thousand containers running at any given time. During a conference a speaker mentioned that in production they had over 4000 containers, but only 400 engineers, meaning that each engineer was responsible for 10 production systems. This would be considered a problem for an API Gateway, since in the current stance most gateways are hand registering each service it communicates with and how to handle the requests to each service (security and traffic policies).

With this massive growth in the number of containers a company creates, container orchestration evolved to start enabling service meshes. The term service mesh is often used to describe the network of microservices that make up such applications and the interactions between them. With the evolution of service meshes to orchestrate the number of containers connected in a logical service, the need to automatically register them into a gateway was desirable. **Istio** was developed as an orchestration tool to manage service meshes as well as **Envoy**.

There is definitely some overlap between API Gateway and Service mesh patterns, i.e. request routing, composition, authentication, rate limiting, error handling, monitoring, etc. That being said, the purpose of a service mesh is for an internal service-to-service communication with policy enforcement, while an API Gateway is primarily meant for external client-to-service communication. Much like an ESB being used as an API Gateway, a service mesh can be used as an API Gateway, but is more suited to replace the work of an ESB and work along side the API Gateway to expose the services to external consumers.

Sidecar Gateways

A trending pattern across all technology is the component movement. In this movement each and everything developed is analyzed to be either a component or a high-order component that is composed of several components. These components are the building blocks of modern applications. This component-based software engineering (CBSE) has even found its way into, what normally is centralized infrastructure, the API Gateway space. This pattern allows an application to get the primary functions of an API Gateway while living side-by-side, instead of having a historical top-down infrastructure. This approach to things allows a distributed method to enforce policies that are at an organization level.

Some examples of sidecar gateways would be **Ambassador**, **Istio**, and even **Kong** has adopted the sidecar approach as a capability.

API First: Weathering the storm

API first design is a strategy in which the first order of business is to develop an API that puts the target developer's interests first and then build the product on top of it (website, mobile application, or a SaaS software).

This design strategy allows the product to enable full flexibility in how the users (developers) decide to utilize the product. This use may be outside the scope that it was designed for, but because of the flexibility new use cases are continually discovered. This strategy is taken into consideration by many engineers in software, construction, and more. Let's take primitive shelters, for example. Their intended use was to allow humans to weather the natural elements. Eventually humans started using shelter to house their possessions, which was outside the provided use case for shelter, but didn't violate the design aspects of a shelter. This use case for shelter led to a redesigning of the house to add more functionality without leaving its original intent behind as a shelter used to weather the natural elements.

To simplify, think about it like this: You built a primitive shelter, and it protects you from the natural elements. The world is a warmer and dryer place.

Now, another person in your tribe starts building an attached room, which interacts with your shelter. Then a third person sees the warmth and dryness the shelter is providing and decides to build a second story to your shelter. Soon, you have multiple people all building attachments with horizontal dependencies that are all on a different build cadence. What can happen if no discipline is applied to this in the realm of APIs is a nightmare of integration failures.

To avoid these integration failures and to recognize your shelter as a first-class artifact of the build process, you'd like others to be able to work against the shelter design contract without interfering with the original space that was developed.

Summary

You know have good examples of the use of API Gateways and why you would want to use Kong. In the next chapter we will look more closely at Kong and also compare it with competing API Gateways that are available.

Kong: API Gateway disruptor 3

Kong is a scalable, open source API Layer (also known as an API Gateway, or API Middleware). To be more precise, Kong is a Lua application running in Nginx that leverages the **lua-nginx-module**. To get the most out of the lua-nginx-module, Kong decided to integrate with **OpenResty** instead of directly compiling Kong against the Nginx module. OpenResty is not a *fork* of Nginx, but rather a set of libraries and modules to extend the capabilities of Nginx.

This foundation allows Kong to remain extensible via a pluggable architecture with Lua *scripts* (referred to as "plugins") that can be loaded at runtime. Because of this, Kong is seen as a **paragon of microservice architecture**; at its core it implements database abstraction, routing, and plugin management, which leads to a separation of concerns; the backbone of microservice architecture. Plugins can live in separate code bases and be injected anywhere into the request lifecycle, all in a few lines of code. This capability allows Kong to facilitate the *world's* problems, allowing developers to resolve their companies problems while not having a steep learning curve.

All of the code for the sample project in this book can be found **here**.

Kong was originally built at Mashape to secure, manage and extend over 15,000 APIs & Microservices for its API Marketplace, which generates billions of requests per month for over 200,000 developers. Today Kong is used in mission critical deployments at small and large organizations, and here are some characteristics:

- Scalable: Kong easily scales horizontally by simply adding more machines, meaning your platform can handle virtually any load while keeping latency low.
- Modular: Kong can be extended by adding new plugins, which are easily configured through a RESTful Admin API.

- Runs on any infrastructure: Kong runs anywhere. You can deploy Kong in the cloud or on-premise environments, including single or multi-datacenter setups and for public, private or invite-only APIs.

API Centric

Most API Gateways are not built with an API first design.

There is the perspective that users only want to interact with beautiful user interfaces and the workings under the hood should be abstracted away from them. This may be true for the general public, who just want to consume the service, but it is a bit of a stretch for the technologically fluent users. Many gateways only ship with a dashboard (**tyk.io**), an application to *craft* the configuration (**KrakenD**) instead of exposing an API to let the user decide how to configure/consume its offerings, or they have both characteristiscs, but lack simplicity (**IBM API Connect**,**APIGEE**).

Kong was built with the API first design pattern allowing users to leverage what they have available in new and exciting ways for the problem that they have to solve for their business. It's also decoupled some of the concerns gateways try to solve out of the box when the box is loosely defined. An example would be service discovery, where there are several methods and products to do service discovery (etcd, istio, linkerd, consult, etc.) and a lot of the gateways try to facilitate this functionality, but generally choose one over the other as an opinion causing the users to also choose that dependency when they may have already setup another system. Kong alleviates this by having everything they do internally exposed as an API, which allows the users to build their own hooks or rely on the community to build hooks for these differently defined boxes.

With this design pattern, many great things come for free for Kong Inc (previously Mashape LLC.) from the **community** such as a User Interface to administer Kong named **Konga**, SDKs (**.Net**, **Java**) and **plugins**.

Open Sourced

Open source software (OSS) is crowd-sourced. As a result it has benefits: cost, flexibility, freedom, security, and accountability, which are unsurpassed by propriety software solutions. Moreover, OSS has long-term viability and is always on the cutting-edge of technology. It is created and supported by a worldwide community of organizations and individual developers, many of whom also live by open source values like collaboration and volunteerism.

The cost benefit alone makes OSS highly appealing. The vast majority of OSS is freely distributed. But OSS is said to be "free as in kittens" and not "free as in beer"—it requires maintenance, configuration, and ongoing support.

The trade-off is flexibility and freedom. Unlike closed proprietary software, OSS can be altered and extended by any developer familiar with the source code. This grants organizations freedom from "vendor lock-in" and assures long-term viability. A widely adopted OSS project is often supported by hundreds of capable development shops that can always be called upon long into the future.

Kong Inc. has made their API Gateway core open source as they want the benefit of having a following of developers to improve the platform and add capabilities that they couldn't achieve with just their developers. This far outweighs the profit of running a purely proprietary API Gateway as users can try it out for free then promote it to their businesses driving more adoption in the market. Although their core foundation is free, software is not cheap so Kong Inc. has found a happy medium by offering *extras* in their enterprise edition (EE), such as plugins like OAuth2 Introspection, Canary Releases, and benefits like an integrated admin UI with Analytics. However their *extras* are just code into the core, which means they can be recreated by the users (**OAuth2 OSS Introspection**).

CONFIGURABLE

Since Kong is using Nginx under the hood, an organization can take their existing Nginx configuration and embed it into Kong's configuration. This allows organizations to ease into the an API gateway without losing all of their existing working configurations. With this capability Kong allows users to leverage features of Nginx that may not be baked into Kong such as HTTP/2.

A common use case for organizations is to serve up a website (**https://example.com**) and an API (**https://example.com/api/**) on the same server. Kong is able to facilitate this by using a custom Nginx configuration template that uses `nginx_kong.lua` and adds a new location block for serving the website alongside the Kong proxy location information. Here is an example:

```
http {
# Kong's Proxy server block
  server {
    server_name kong;

    # any contents until the location / block
    ...

    # here, we declare our custom location serving our
website
    # (or API portal) which we can optimize for serving
static assets
    location / {
      root /var/www/example.com;
      index index.htm index.html;
      ...
    }

    # Kong's Proxy location / has been changed to /api
    location /api {
      set $upstream_host nil;
      set $upstream_scheme nil;
      set $upstream_uri nil;

      # Any remaining configuration for the Proxy location
      ...
    }
  }
}
```

Along with being able to use a custom Nginx configuration, Kong also enables a configuration file (default location: `/etc/kong/kong.conf.default`). This configuration file can be overridden by using the `-c / --conf` flag on startup.

Here is a preview of some defaults:

```
prefix = /usr/local/kong/
log_level = notice
proxy_access_log = logs/access.log
proxy_error_log = logs/error.log
admin_access_log = logs/admin_access.log
admin_error_log = logs/error.log
custom_plugins = NONE
anonymous_reports = on
proxy_listen = 0.0.0.0:8000
proxy_listen_ssl = 0.0.0.0:8443
admin_listen = 127.0.0.1:8001
```

```
admin_listen_ssl = 127.0.0.1:8444
nginx_user = nobody nobody
nginx_worker_processes = auto
nginx_optimizations = on
nginx_daemon = on
mem_cache_size = 128m
http2 = off
```

These configuration values can also be overridden via environment variables. The format for using environment variables is by using the `KONG_` prefix to the setting to override with it being in all capitalized letters. For example the setting `log_level` can be overridden with `KONG_LOG_LEVEL`. These environment variables come in handy when you need to update a storage configuration for a particular environment, but want the rest of the preset configurations.

With organizations being diverse in their storage options (relational databases and noSQL databases) using these environment overrides allows quick settings for your storage options per environment to ensure the easiest transition from lower environments (development, test, etc) to production environments with no changes outside environment overrides.

EXTENSIBILITY (HIGH LEVEL)

Configuration is a valuable asset to any software because it allows the users to bend it to their needs. Kong takes it one step further and allows you to write plugins to fulfill the void that is not readily offered. Many API Gateways come with some staples such as rate limiting, logging, and request transformation, and Kong is no different, but it also offers many more plugins out of the gate such as:

- Basic Authentication
- Key Authentication
- OAuth 2.0 Authentication
- HMAC Authentication
- JWT
- LDAP Authentication
- ACL
- CORS
- Dynamic SSL
- IP Restriction
- Bot Detection

- Request Size Limiting
- Rate Limiting
- Response Rate Limiting
- Request Termination
- AWS Lambda
- OpenWhisk
- Galileo
- Datadog
- Runscope
- Request Transformer
- Response Transformer
- Correlation ID
- TCP
- UDP
- HTTP
- File
- StatsD
- Syslog
- Loggly

Along with the provided plugins there are many open source plugins that are available to fulfill what is missing in Kong's offering for particular problems. These plugins can generally be found from searching the **Luarocks** repository. A good example of the community solving a problem with a plugin that is not offered in the community edition is an **OAuth2 Introspection plugin**.

Plugins being developed, and the ability to interact with the core of the gateway is an example of how the ability to develop plugins can solve business problems. A plugin can alleviate some network congestion by doing pre-fetching of data, such as a users profile, and loading it into the gateway cache while adding it to the upstream headers. In this scenario a plugin can reduce the network congestion because it checks the cache and only fetches the profile data based on a TTL (Time To Live). This pre-fetching capability reduces network congestion by 10x or greater because several API's may require this information. Previously they would each have to make this call instead of just reading the data from the headers.

To aide in the development of plugins the Kong developers have documented a guide on building plugins as well as producing a project seed that we will talk about later in this book.

Enterprise Edition: API platform

Software is not cheap by any means because you have to pay developers, pay marketing to get it out in the wild, and pay for support personnel if you want to be a differentiator in a market. KongHQ has not only enhanced their community edition of their API Gateway software, but with their Enterprise Edition they provide an API Platform.

WHAT IS AN API PLATFORM

An API Platform is more than just an API Gateway, since it contains all of the pieces to the puzzle that enable an organization to hit the ground running while exposing API's to their consumers. The classic API Platform features are an API gateway, a developer portal, and a management portal. Without offering an API platform most organizations will not want to build all of these missing pieces because they see them as expensive and not a differentiator for their core business.

API GATEWAY

Instead of walling off the capabilities of their software, KongHQ (formerly Mashape Inc) decided to build their Enterprise Edition (EE) off the core of the Community Edition (CE). By doing this there are a few features that are not available in Kong CE that have been released only under the Kong EE. Some of these plugins are just enhanced counterparts to their CE versions, while others are new plugins. The list will continue to grow as KongHQ finds more business needs to solve for organizations that will pay the premium.

Here is a preview of EE only plugins:

- OpenID Connect 1.0 RP - OpenID Connect (1.0) plugin allows the integration with a 3rd party identity provider (IdP) or Kong OAuth 2.0 Plugin in a standardized way.
- OAuth 2.0 Introspection - Validate access tokens sent by developers using a third-party OAuth 2.0 Authorization Server, by leveraging its Introspection Endpoint (RFC 7662). This plugin assumes that the Consumer already has an access token that will be validated against a third-party OAuth 2.0 server.
- Canary Release - Reduce the risk of introducing a new software version in production by slowly rolling out the change to a small subset of users. This plugin also enables roll back to your original upstream service, or shift all traffic to the new version.

- Forward Proxy - The Forward Proxy plugin allows Kong to connect to intermediary transparent HTTP proxies, instead of directly to the upstream_url, when forwarding requests upstream. This is useful in environments where Kong sits in an organization's internal network, because the upstream API is available via the public Internet, and the organization proxies all outbound traffic through a forward proxy server.
- Proxy Caching - The Proxy Caching plugin for Kong Enterprise Edition makes it fast and easy to configure caching of responses and serving of those cached responses to matching requests.
- Rate Limiting *(Enhanced)* - The Rate Limiting plugin for Kong Enterprise Edition is a re-engineered version of the incredibly popular Community Edition Rate Limiting plugin, with greatly enhanced configuration options and performance.
- Request Transformer *(Enhanced)* - The Request Transformer plugin for Kong Enterprise Edition builds on the Community Edition version of this plugin with enhanced capabilities to match portions of incoming requests using regular expressions, save those matched strings into variables, and substitute those strings into transformed requests via flexible templates.

Along with the additional plugins and enhanced plugins, the EE also comes with the other parts of an API Platform that are missing with the CE. These missing parts of an API Platform are the Developer Portal and the Administration Portal.

DEVELOPER PORTAL

An organization has an API Gateway that exposes their API's to the world to consume, however, where does the documentation live? Usually the documentation is handled via a Developer Portal, which will not only allow consumers to register an application (if using OAuth2) or request any API Key (using the `key-auth` plugin), but it also presents the documentation of the APIs in a clean and crisp format with code samples on how to invoke the APIs.

There are many open source solutions to display documentation, but the management portal and cohesion between the gateway and documentation is generally lacking. While many other solutions offer half-baked documentation solutions (most use an instance of Drupal) KongHQ has embedded their developer portal software with the EE of their API Gateway. This allows features to be developed directly against the API Gateway providing that cohesion to allow things such as automatic discovery and auditing when APIs are published without documentation.

MANAGEMENT PORTAL

We talked earlier about how Kong was "API Centric," and while many developers prefer to work in automated ways using tools like curl/postman/httpie to make their configuration changes, not all users of Kong are developers. In fact many users of Kong are infrastructure groups that may understand/utilize the APIs directly, but they may only have the talent pool to only use this side of the configuration. Knowing the industry KongHQ's EE offers a Management Portal that allows Role Based Access Control (RBAC) security with a user interface to allow even non-technical people access to view, enable, and understand the health of the API Platform. Although KongHQ created a management portal for the EE, some users of the CE were missing this capability as well, which lead to the creation of the **Konga Dashboard**. This dashboard can be leveraged to achieve the same level of management without paying for the EE.

What is it disrupting?

Disruptive innovation is a term in the field of business administration that refers to an innovation that creates a new market and value network and eventually disrupts an existing market and value network. It also displaces established market leading firms, products, and alliances. Currently, the leaders in the API Gateway space are Apigee, IBM with API Connect, Mashery, and Mulesoft. KongHQ is becoming a disruptor in this space by offering a high quality API Gateway that is customizable and flexible without the high cost of these leaders.

Kong is an API Gateway at heart, while becoming an API Platform for a premium. Although their API Platform offerings are still new, they are bringing a lot of features to this space that are lacking. This section, however, will be focusing on the capabilities of the API Gateway and not the platform as a whole. In this section we will focus on some open source competitors, as well as some licenses alternatives. We will be analyzing these at face value without customizations and without specialized training on each one (knowing the ins and outs of configurations, setup, etc). Through this analysis we will demonstrate why Kong is being a disruptor in the space of API Gateways. We will specifically talk about the Gateway, not the dev portal/analytics that each of these offer.

To begin let's list the core attributes of an API Gateway that makes or breaks one from being a leader.

- Cost - Cost is a big considerations because it drives whether an organization only uses the API Gateway for external consumers or if they use it across the organization for all communications.
- API Configuration - How configurable is the API Gateway? How is it configured (file, environment, API, etc.)? How are configurations enabled (via a reload, restart, or live)?
- Installation - What are the requirements, dependencies, and difficulty setting up the gateway? On-premise or cloud?
- Customizability - API Gateways solve the worlds problems but not every organization's problems. How easy can an organization customize the gateway to solve their problems?
- Community - Without a community organization, you must rely solely on paid support to aide with questions using a solution. Is the community active? What forms of communication are available (chat, email, forum, etc.)?

Kong

- Cost -
  - Open Source (free)
  - Paid Enterprise version
- Configuration:
  - Simple REST API with almost immediate (based on the database polling setting for multi-node setups) results
- Installation:
  - 14 methods of installation ranging from the source code, package managers (`apt-get`, `homebrew`, etc), containerization deployments (`docker`, `kubernetes`, `DC/OS`) to prepackaged cloud setups (`AWS Cloud Formation`, `AWS Marketplace`, `Google Cloud Platform`). These methods and instructions can be found on **KongHQ.com**.
  - Kong requires a Cassandra or Postgres database to store the configuration. Once a Kong node has been started and configuration has been loaded, it can lose connectivity with its datastore and still function without any authentication keys that are already loaded into cache.
- Customizability:
  - Custom Nginx Configuration
  - Envrionment Overrides

    - Custom Plugins are encouraged and provided via the community. **Guides** are available from KongHQ as well as examples as their core plugins are open-sourced.
- Community:
    - Active community on **forums**, as well as participating in the chat systems (**Gitter** - ***deprecated***, **IRC** - **#kong**)
    - Community developed plugins
    - Over 14,000 github stars
- Overview:
    - Free / Cheap EE price models
    - Customizable and configurable to an organizations environment.
    - API First mentality for configuration and development.
    - Minimal dependencies
    - Multitude of installation options from cloud to on-premise.

Overall, Kong is considered the cream of the crop in terms of an API Gateway for its flexibility to conform to the environment it's being used in.

Tyk.io

- Cost:
    - On-premise
        - Free for 1 node
        - £6000/yr for 2 nodes
    - Cloud:
        - Starting at £200/mo for 1 million API Calls
- Configuration:
    - File driven design per node
    - Verbose REST API that only reconfigures a file after a hot-reload must be initiated to reload the node configuration.
- Installation:
    - Available via `Docker`, `Red Hat (RHEL)`, `Ubuntu` and `Source`
    - Components: Tyk.io is broken into several components that each have to be running and configured.
        - Tyk Pump
        - Tyk Dashboard
        - Tyk Gateway

  - Dependencies:
    - Redis
    - Mongo
- Customizability:
  - Plugins in a variety of languages (JS, Lua, Python, gRPC)
  - Error templates can be modified for a pleasant experience.
- Community:
  - **Forums**
- Overview:
  - Tyk.io boast that it is open source, yet you have to obtain a *FREE* license to utilize a single node. This is an upsell tactic that will get companies hooked into a vendor lock-in scenario forcing their hand to buy the software.
  - Tyk.io is a file driven gateway that has verbose APIs that simply update a configuration on a node. When running hundreds of nodes this doesn't seem manageable.
  - Tyk.io has many components and requirements to get up and running. Although it is an API Platform, and not just a gateway, it has a high barrier to entry to even begin.

KrakenD

- Cost:
  - Free and Open Source
- Configuration:
  - Configured via a file. An online editor is provided to make generating these files easier
- Installation -
  - Available via `Docker`, `Debian & Ubuntu`, `CentOS, Fedora, Red Hat (RHEL)`, `Mac OSX` and `Source`
  - No dependencies
- Customizability:
  - Written as a Framework to build your own gateway!
  - Written in Go
- Community:
  - **Blog**
  - **Twitter**
- Overview:
  - One of the fatest API gateways in the market.

    - Built as a framework to enable building your own gateway
    - File based configuration per node with no managed clustering without paying the premium.
    - Configurations built via an editor to generate a configuration file, can become unmanageable with thousands of nodes.

Apigee

- Cost:
    - Basic: 3 user, 2 environments $5000/yr with 15 million API Calls per month.
    - Business: 5 user, 3 environments $25,000/yr with 300 million API Calls per month.
- Configuration -
    - An XML API is available to configuration.
    - Proprietary routing syntax
- Installation:
    - Basic is only available in the cloud with a microgateway available on premise which requires access to the cloud servers for configuration.
- Customizability:
    - Custom proxies can be added to the flow for additional customizations. These proxies can be a NodeJS application.
- Community:
    - **Forums**
    - **Academy - Tutorials/Training**
- Overview:
    - Apigee is a full API Platform without the ability to just have an API Gateway.
    - On-premise requires access to cloud resources to obtain configurations.
    - Costs for some organizations are too expensive to justify, as not only do they have to pay for people to have training in Apigee, but any customizations via NodeJS proxies will have to have developer effort, which adds to the cost.

IBM API Connect

- Cost:

    - Unknown - We were unable to find a price online however evaluation is free.
- Configuration:
    - Much like Apigee it seems that IBM's API Connects an XML API is available for configuration using a proprietary syntax for routing.
    - Configurations on premise require a Datapower instance on premise or over the Internet.
- Installation:
    - Components:
        - Cloud Management Console (cmc)
        - API Management (apim)
    - Available via `VMWare`, `Citrix` or `Docker`
- Customizability:
    - Much like Apigee, customization can be provided via NodeJS applications.
- Community:
    - **Forums**
    - **Academy, Tutorials, Resources**
- Overview:
    - IBM's API Connect seems to be an *enterprise* familiar vendor version of Apigee. Each feature is almost like-for-like in both platforms.
    - IBM's API Connect is a full API Platform and cannot be run just as a single gateway.

With the analysis being broken down it shows that KongHQ had a vision to be the easiest to manage, while being the most flexible API Gateway in the market built on proven and widely used technology. While taking storm in the open source market, it has also been disrupting the market share of some of the *enterprise* ready solutions with its flexibility and ease of setup. Since most of the *enterprise* ready solutions are API Platforms and not just API Gateways, it is even more impressive that the Kong CE API Gateway is growing in popularity compared to these solutions, since it is only one piece to the puzzle of running an API Initiative for an organization.

Summary

We have analyzed what makes Kong CE a great solution and compared it to other open source and off the shelf solutions in terms of an API Gateway. Now let's go through the Kong architecture to demonstrate how the software works to provide a deeper understanding of why this is becoming a disruptor.

Kong architecture 4

The Kong website displays **a great getting started section** that includes in three steps how to register a new API and start requesting it. You can really consider (read **buy**) Kong API gateway as a blackbox:

- Setup the API gateway
- Tweak the configuration through the HTTP interface to target your APIs
- Direct traffic to Kong with the right headers

And that is a very good thing about the project. Being able sometimes to outsource most of the work to focus on more different features for your business makes a lot of sense.

But you might also want to understand what's going on with your requests. Perhaps you are not comfortable with blackboxes manipulating all of your sensitive requests. Or maybe you need more than the available plugins to develop a new one. Or perhaps your application is under edge conditions and it makes sense to understand the underlying logic to make a better usage of the project.

The following sections should give you the framework you need, whatever the use case.

All of the code for the sample project in this book can be found **here**.

Overall approach and black box description

If you know how to bootstrap and configure Kong, you basically have a magic service that takes requests as input, routes it to the right service, and gives you back a response.

Along the way the gorilla gets full access and control over this request, transforming or analyzing its attributes.

From this very high level perspective you can see the shape of Kong's benefits for cloud architectures. All of the common features you can expect, or wish, from modern APIs can be refactored into one separate layer. No need to reimplement your **JWT authentification**, given both your payment API in Python and your events server in Scala. Do it once, deploy once. And remove some duplicate boilerplate. No more rate limiting code close to business logic or data modelization issues.

Kong unlocks very powerful architectural patterns. But that's exactly what we won't develop or study. That is a topic for another time because we have much to explore into the architecture of Kong itself. Indeed we are going back to lower levels and will dive into the details of how Kong handles requests. No matter where it goes, and from where it came, we will try to understand the how and why of what happens to those requests.

I hope it will provide you with the wisdom to move forward and understand under the right lights the other sections of this book. There's no blackbox, no magic, just cautious choices and considerations for real-life challenges.

Now let's move on and dissect the project like hardware hackers.

The HTTP server blocks

When tackling new frameworks or technologies in 2018 you are often offeredthe choice to either use the project right away, thanks to **Docker**, or to build it from source. The latter option is usually barely documented and barely useful, except for some low level customization that needs to recompile the project. But I believe this is actually a powerful approach to learn more about the project internals.

The project is 99.8% made of **lua** scripts, and you can quickly understand why reaching to the **official install from source section**. Step 1 states right away that Kong is an **OpenResty** application, which is itself an extension of Nginx. So Kong stands on a giant's shoulders. Or more precisely it is *composed* of giants. Let's start from the beginning and understand this design.

Nginx can be extended by Lua scripts through the `ngx_lua module`, which you can compile to native C code that can integrate with Nginx Sources. OpenResty builds on top of this and bundles a **consistent set of modules** along with Nginx itself to offer a powerful and extensible webserver for HTTP intensive applications. The two projects maintain a close relationship, with Nginx merging sometimes OpenResty modules into its upstream source. As Thibault Charbonnier **explains it on Quora**:

> At Mashape, we wanted to build a modulable reverse proxy (on top of Nginx) that would handle features that are common between APIs (authentication, logging, rate-limiting...). We had two ways to do that: by bundling Nginx with our own flavour of 3rd party modules (the said plugins), or by developing on top of OpenResty.
> We admired the work done on OpenResty and thought of a way to build a modulable core, on which plugins could be added. Hence, Kong is mostly a collection of Lua scripts that allow it to add services (APIs...) at runtime, and the execution of plugins on top of those.

The answer was written on Oct 17, 2015 and 2 years later it proved to be a successful approach. The project is thriving in demanding production environments, building upon Nginx strengths and OpenResty extensibility. Core maintainers and developers can focus on developing *features that are common between APIs*, while the foundations handle high performance non-blocking HTTP traffic handling.

Relying on OpenResty also helps developers writing Kong plugin because their Lua API is accessible within the script. The **bot-detector** plugin for example imports a very common **LRU Cache** with components directly from [OpenResty library][modules].

```
local lrucache = require "resty.lrucache"

-- per-worker cache of matched UAs
-- we use a weak table, index by the `conf` parameter, so
once the
plugin config
-- is GC'ed, the cache follows automatically
local ua_caches = setmetatable({}, { __mode = "k" })
local UA_CACHE_SIZE = 10 ^ 4

-- [ ... ]

function BotDetectionHandler:access(conf)
    -- [ ... ]
    local cache = ua_caches[conf]
  if not cache then
      cache = lrucache.new(UA_CACHE_SIZE)
    ua_caches[conf] = cache
  end

    local match  = cache:get(user_agent)
    if not match then
        match = examine_agent(user_agent, conf)
        cache:set(user_agent, match)
    end
```

```
    -- [ ... ]
end

return BotDetectionHandler
```

A few lines of scripting and you just implemented a useful caching system for your plugin.

But Kong also brings this HTTP admin interface that makes the whole proxy dynamic and transforms the static webserver into an adaptable API Gateway.

Look back at the installation page and after compiling Kong lua sources, you're asked to prepare a database. **Cassandra 3.x.x** and **Postgresql 9.5+** are supported but for what purpose exactly? Let's move on to the next section and figure this out.

Database and high level blocks

Put simply, Kong needs to remember a lot of details along its lifecycle and store them between requests to provide a consistent behavior. We can distinguish between three kinds of scenarios where data ends up stored in a relational database:

- **APIs management through the admin interface**
- **Kong internals and clustering**
- **Custom plugins behavior**

Let's take a concrete look at what's inside an initialized Kong cluster (i.e. Kong started and the database was migrated).

As a convenient example we use below a Postgres datastore assuming the reader is comfortable with basic SQL queries. It is important to remember, like mentioned above, that Kong supports a second datastore backend: Apache Cassandra.

Given your infrastructure and production constraints you might consider using one or the other. When Kong is used in a multi-region, multi data-center, high-availability environment, Cassandra is usually the preferred choice, because a distribute setup is built into its core.

In a nutshell, the columnar database is indeed designed to use many commodity servers distributed across several data centers to handle large amounts of data without a single point of failure. Every single node of the cluster is considered identical (masterless) and data is replicated automatically to multiple nodes, for fault-tolerance.

To tease your curiosity and illustrate, here are a few examples of CQL (Cassadra Query Language):

```
cqlsh> create keyspace demo with replication =
{'class':'SimpleStrategy','replication_factor' : 2};
cqlsh> use demo;
cqlsh:demo> create table api (apiid int primary key, apiname
varchar);
cqlsh:demo> insert into api (apiid, apiname) values (1,
'Mortgages');
cqlsh:demo> update api set apiname = 'Loans' where apiid = 1;
cqlsh:demo> select * from api where apiid = 1;
 apiid | apiname
-------+---------
     1 |   Loans

(1 rows)
```

Back to our initial setup with a Kong instance and a PostgreSQL data backend. Let's inspect the internal memory of our fresh Gateway.

```
(kpler) kong :: (tech/kong*) » pgcli -h localhost --
user=kong --password
Password:
Version: 1.4.0
Chat: https://gitter.im/dbcli/pgcli
Mail: https://groups.google.com/forum/#!forum/pgcli
Home: http://pgcli.com
kong@localhost:kong> \d
+----------+-------------------------------+--------
+---------+
| Schema   | Name                          | Type   |
Owner   |
|----------+-------------------------------+--------
+---------|
| public   | acls                          | table  |
kong    |
| public   | apis                          | table  |
kong    |
| public   | basicauth_credentials         | table  |
kong    |
| public   | cluster_events                | table  |
kong    |
| public   | consumers                     | table  |
kong    |
| public   | hmacauth_credentials          | table  |
kong    |
| public   | jwt_secrets                   | table  |
```

```
kong     |
| public   | keyauth_credentials           | table  |
kong     |
| public   | oauth2_authorization_codes    | table  |
kong     |
| public   | oauth2_credentials            | table  |
kong     |
| public   | oauth2_tokens                 | table  |
kong     |
| public   | plugins                       | table  |
kong     |
| public   | ratelimiting_metrics          | table  |
kong     |
| public   | response_ratelimiting_metrics | table  |
kong     |
| public   | schema_migrations             | table  |
kong     |
| public   | ssl_certificates              | table  |
kong     |
| public   | ssl_servers_names             | table  |
kong     |
| public   | targets                       | table  |
kong     |
| public   | ttls                          | table  |
kong     |
| public   | upstreams                     | table  |
kong     |
+----------+-------------------------------+--------
+---------+
SELECT 20
```

At this stage everything is pretty much empty, but we can spot the three mentioned categories. Let's try to add a new API like the **quick-start guide** suggests.

```
$ # let's register a new API
$ curl -i -X POST \
  --url http://localhost:8001/apis/ \
  --data 'name=example-api' \
  --data 'hosts=example.com' \
  --data 'upstream_url=http://mockbin.org'

$ # and enable a 'basic auth' plugin for this API
```

And without any surprise, Kong stores this information to handle future requests.

```
kong@localhost:kong> SELECT name, hosts, upstream_url FROM
apis
+-------------+-----------------+--------------------+
| name        | hosts           | upstream_url       |
|-------------+-----------------+--------------------|
| example-api | ["example.com"] | http://mockbin.org |
+-------------+-----------------+--------------------+

kong@localhost:kong> SELECT a.name as api, a.upstream_url,
p.name as plugin, p.enabled
FROM plugins p, apis a
WHERE p.api_id = a.id
+-------------+--------------------+----------+-----------+
| api         | upstream_url       | plugin   | enabled   |
|-------------+--------------------+----------+-----------|
| example-api | http://mockbin.org | key-auth | True      |
+-------------+--------------------+----------+-----------+
```

Everything you can control through the admin API is stored. It allows multiple Kong instances to share the same state of the Gateway and therefore to scale horizontally (it is actually more complex than that, but we will get there). Kong can even crash and restart without losing its configuration.

Kong's data layer is a good way to wrap up the high level components that collaborate to handle incoming requests.

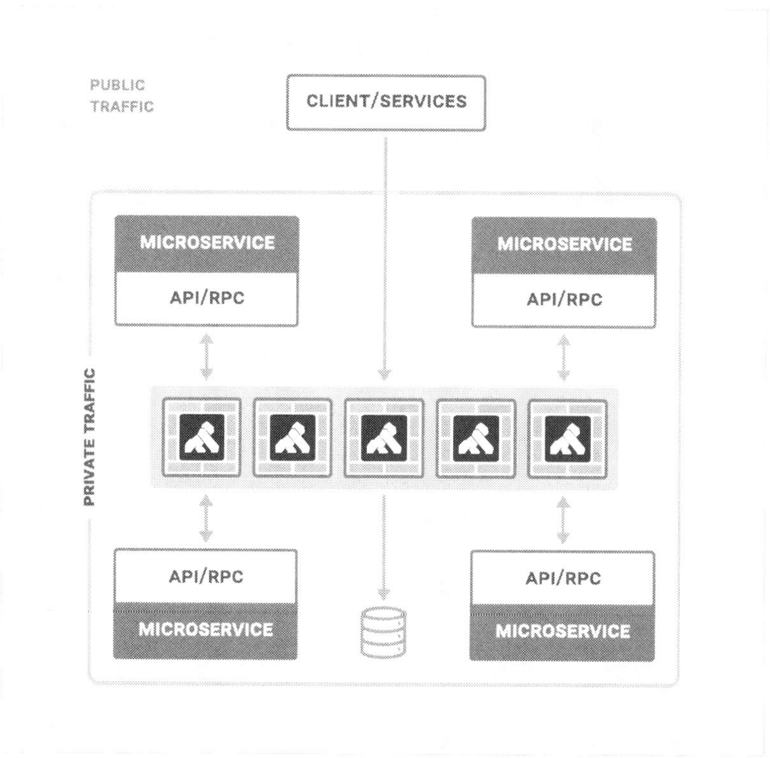

Let's take the schema above to help us walk through the tech once again. Assuming a production setup, we start several instances of Kong for failover and redundancy. We still need a load balancer to distribute traffic among the nodes, so we also start Nginx or **Haproxy** in front of them.

Of course, we have APIs distributed around an operator configuring Kong to route the HTTP traffic, sent by consumers. All of this setup is stored in Cassandra or Postgres by the Gateway and every nodes share it. It makes the data store a single pont of failure so a realistic and cautious production environment will deploy them with failover capabilities.

So we went from a Kong blackbox to a composition of blocks that should give you a better sense of the underlying technologies and philosophies. In the next section we will dig deeper into how Kong (the library) uses those elements to decide what to do with incoming traffic.

Requests/response path

We saw in the previous sections the critical technological choices made and part of their rational. Something Kong brags a lot about is its real life deployment in high-intensive environments. Although relying on very concurrent and fast stacks (like NGINX), an API Gateway is a critical path by nature. It should be as reliable, as best known practices suggest, and that is why Kong's authors implemented some high-availibility and fail-over mechanisms.

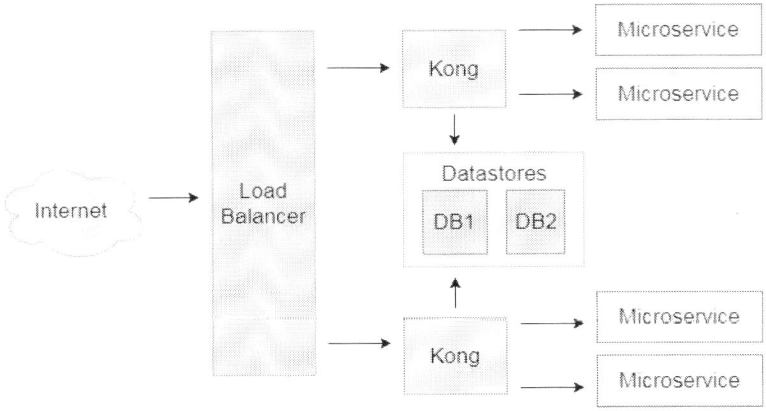

But before forcing users to horizontally scale their fleet of gateways (and their bill), Mashape implemented some sound optimizations to avoid unecessary computing or i/o roundtrips.

Kong uses a cache in memory to minimize access to the database. All the entities such as APIs, Plugins or Consumers are cached in memory.

Previous versions of the software used `Serf` as a mechanism to notify to other members of the Kong cluster that a change was done in the datastore so those nodes were able to update their caches. With older versions, it was common to use ports such as 7946 and 7373 to notify invalidation events.

Now, Kong uses a completely different strategy. All nodes perform a periodic background job to check if configuration changes have been received and processed by other Kong nodes.

This table summarizes the parameters that control how the invalidation mechanism should work:

Parameter	Default	Description
db_update_frequency	5	Controls the frequency that will use Kong to search for changes in the database. The smaller the value, the more often the different nodes will apply the configuration changes.
db_update_propagation	0	Useful when Cassandra is used as a datastore. As Cassandra is eventually consistent, that means that not all Cassandra nodes will contain the latest changes of configuration. When this parameter is set, Kong nodes will wait for db_update_propagations seconds to update their cache.
db_cache_ttl	3600	This parameter controls how long a value is stored on the cache. This mechanism acts as a safeguard to guarantee that in case a node misses an invalidation event, that node will end reading again the configuration from the database after db_cache_ttl seconds.

Summary

Running Kong internals through X-Ray gave us some useful clues. The project is a composition of battle-tested technologies, and some of them can be swapped, like the datastore, leaving some flexibility to production deployments.

Already this is something constructive for sceptical DevOps. We also had a glimpse at some performance optimization the Gorilla implements, giving us the keys to evaluate the project against business needs. The time invested in understanding what happens to HTTP requests will also shine when debugging complex network scenarios, or scaling APIs to high workloads (the very worst we can wish for a growing a business).

A lot of promises... but right now, it should help us tackle the rest of this book.

Meet the Kong 5

Before diving into this chapter, it's necessary to prepare a microservice API. As mentioned earlier in **Chapter 1 - Microservices architecture**, we introduced a simple cinema microservice.

Example: Setting up a simple microservice (Cinema3)

Cinema 3 is an extremely simplified example of microservices in Python. It demonstrates the use of microservices for a fictional movie theater. `Cinema 3`'s backend is constructed with four microservices, and each microservice is built on top of **Flask**, a micro web framework written in Python.

Microservice	Endpoint	Description
Movie Service	/movies, /movies/{id}	Information like movie ratings, title, etc.
Show Times Service	/showtimes, /showtimes/{date}	Show times information.
Booking Service	/bookings, /bookings/{user}	Booking information.
Users Service	/users, /users/{user}	Movie suggestions for users by communicating with other services.

Here, we'll use `docker-compose` to run each microservice. If you don't have **docker-compose**, please install it before you start.

To make Cinema 3 run on your host, clone it with `git` in your working directory and run with `docker-compose`.

```
git clone https://github.com/backstopmedia/kong-book-example
cinema-3
cd cinema-3
docker-compose up
 # docker-compose will show you logs of active request to
your services.
```

To check that your service is running properly, issue `http://localhost:8080/movies` with curl.

```
curl http://localhost:8080/movies
```

```
{
    "267eedb8-0f5d-42d5-8f43-72426b9fb3e6": {
        "director": "Ryan Coogler",
        "id": "267eedb8-0f5d-42d5-8f43-72426b9fb3e6",
        "rating": 8.8,
        "title": "Creed"
    },
...... output truncated ......
```

We've just created our first microservice! From now on, we'll use this example with each Kong feature.

Starting Kong

Kong is used with lots of use-cases and due to this, configuring Kong will be diverse. For example, let's assume that you're in start-up and planning for the simple usage of API Gateway. For this you'll be fine with the default Kong configuration with a `Postgresql` Datastore. But if you're in enterprise and planning for the complex usage of the API Gateway, such as multi-dc deployment or high-availability, using a `Cassandra`-based datastore is more efficient due to `Cassandra`'s powerful performance with the distributed environment.

In this section, we're going to look over how to configure Kong with diverse uses. We'll point out how to install and configure Kong, set up a datastore, secure Kong, and customize Nginx.

Install & Configure Kong

Kong can be installed in various ways, such as Ubuntu, RHEL, Docker, Kubernetes, Vagrant, etc. Details about installation with each vendor can be found **here**.

From here, we'll use `Ubuntu 16.04 Xenial` to install and start Kong.

To install Kong on your host, first, download **Kong-Ubuntu** and execute the command.

```
 # Download with curl, if your running on headless host
 # curl -L -O -J https://bintray.com/kong/kong-community-
edition-deb/download_file?file_path=dists/kong-community-
edition-0.12.1.xenial.all.deb
sudo apt-get update
sudo apt-get install openssl libpcre3 procps perl
sudo dpkg -i kong-community-edition-0.12.1.*.deb
```

Issuing those commands doesn't mean you succeed with running Kong. Before starting up, configuring Kong is recommended. If no configuration is provided, it uses a default configuration located at `/etc/kong/kong.conf.default`.

Kong provides two options to configure:

- Configure with a custom configuration file

To start with a custom configuration, copy and modify `kong.conf.default`, and run Kong with the `--conf` option

```
cp /etc/kong/kong.conf.default kong.conf
 # Configure your 'kong.conf' file.
kong start --conf </path/to/kong.conf>
```

After configuring your own `kong.conf`, you can verify it with the `check` command.

```
kong check <path/to/kong.conf>
configuration at <path/to/kong.conf> is valid
```

- Configure with the environment variable

If you only want to modify the configuration slightly, you can configure Kong with environment variables. While Kong loads a configuration, it also looks for environment variables with the same name.

```
export KONG_DATABASE=postgres
kong start
```

The full specification of configuration attributes can be found **here**.

At this point, you might encounter an error, but it's fine. We didn't configure Kong with a datastore.

```
Error: /usr/local/share/lua/5.1/pgmoon/init.lua:271: missing
password, required for connect
======================    OR    ======================
Error: /usr/local/share/lua/5.1/kong/cmd/start.lua:62: /usr/
local/share/lua/5.1/kong/cmd/start.lua:28:
[postgres error] could not retrieve current migrations:
[postgres error] ERROR: permission denied for relation
schema_migrations
```

Setting up a datastore

To start Kong running, datastores needs to be provisioned in order to interact with Kong. Datastores are used by Kong to store API rules, consumers, plugins, cache, etc.

The Kong datastore can be set up with two types of datastores: `PostgreSQL` or `Cassandra`.

- `PostgreSQL` is a widely used relational database system.
  Unlike other RDBMS, it has powerful functionality with managing data.

- `Cassandra` is a partitioned row store based database system (sharding).
  By its architecture it has some advantages with performance and fail-tolerance.
  (Cassandra is optimized for a distributed, high-availability environment.)

(More comparisons between two datastores: **Cassandra vs. PostgreSQL**)

If you're planning to use a single instance or want to keep configuration simple, `PostgreSQL` is the right one for you. But if you're looking forward to dealing with a large amount of distributed deployment, `Cassandra` will fit with your case.

After choosing which datastore to use, provision your database and user for Kong to interact with. For instance, if you are using `PostgreSQL`, issue this command.

```
CREATE USER <PG_USER>;
ALTER USER <PG_USER> with PASSWORD '<PG_PASS>';
CREATE DATABASE <PG_DB> OWNER <PG_USER>;
```

When provisioning a database, configure Kong with a datastore. To configure each type of datastore:

- Configure your `kong.conf` by removing comments on pg or `cassandra`'s prefixed line.

```
# kong.conf
database = postgres
pg_host = <PG_HOST>
pg_database = <PG_DB>
pg_user = <PG_USER>
pg_password = <PG_PASS>
```

- Define environment variables with a KONG prefix.

```
# OR with environment variables
export KONG_DATABASE=postgres
export KONG_CASSANDRA_CONTACT_POINTS=<CASSANDRA_HOST>
export KONG_CASSANDRA_KEYSPACE=<CASSANDRA_KEYSPACE>
export KONG_CASSANDRA_USERNAME=<CASSANDRA_USER>
export KONG_CASSANDRA_PASSWORD=<CASSANDRA_PASSWORD>
```

Now, run the `kong migrations` so that Kong can prepare its own database.

```
kong migrations up [-c /path/to/kong.conf]

migrating core for database kong
core migrated up to: 2015-01-12-175310_skeleton
core migrated up to: 2015-01-12-175310_init_schema
...... output truncated ......
migrating response-transformer for database kong
migrating oauth2 for database kong
oauth2 migrated up to: 2015-08-03-132400_init_oauth2
...... output truncated ......
58 migrations ran
```

And finally, start up your Kong.

```
kong start [-c /path/to/kong.conf]
```

```
Kong started
```

To test if Kong has been started successfully:

```
curl http://localhost:8000/
{"message":"no API found with those values"}
```

Kong started successfully. You are good to go!

Securing Kong

Until now, we've been setting up the basics of Kong. Before we send requests to Kong, we need to secure our requests. Securing Kong with the certificate can be handled in several ways.

- Configure SSL (Certificate handled by Kong)
  Configure Kong with the absolute path of your SSL certificate and SSL Key.
  (If you don't have your certificate, you can issue one with **Certbot** at no cost.)

```
# kong.conf
ssl = on
ssl_cert = <absolute path to the SSL>
ssl_cert_key = <absolute path to the SSL key>
```

If you are using Docker, you can pass SSL certificate with `docker volume (-v option)` or extend a Kong Docker image including an SSL certificate.

- Certificate configured outside of Kong (eg. Load Balancer, CDN, etc.)

If you are using extra endpoints in front of Kong, configuring the certificate and proxying request with it will secure requests to Kong. This method doesn't need to configure any options with Kong. [Must be configured SSL=on (default)]

```
![Secure-LB](images/CH5Figures_Lee/Secure-LB.png)

or example, if you are using cloud provider's Load Balancer
(eg. AWS ELB), it can be secured with SSL certificates (eg.
```

```
AWS Certificate Manager). With this secured Load Balancer,
secured requests can be proxied to Kong.
```

Customize Nginx

Kong is built on top of OpenResty, which is a dynamic web platform based on the Lua script-enabled Nginx.

To understand it further, let's deconstruct Kong into pieces:

Nginx is one of the most popular event-based web servers and load balancers. Its behavior is defined by a configuration-based construct, which means it doesn't support dynamically programmable configurations.

On the other hand, **OpenResty** enables this feature with the **lua-nginx-module**. This module enables developers to extend their Nginx with custom behavior written in Lua. Openresty wraps `Nginx` and `lua-nginx-module` into one package.

And `Kong` is an API Gateway that provides easily applicable extra functionality to backend services by using a RESTful Administration API and plugins.

Due to this architecture, it is highly available to customize or extend Nginx. This means you can tweak your Nginx or extend Kong by adding a new custom server_block.

When `kong starts`, Kong generates a Nginx configuration file at `/usr/local/kong/nginx-kong.conf`. If you need to tweak some of the Nginx configuration, which can't be handled by Kong configuration, you can copy and make your own version and run your own Nginx configuration.

```
kong start -c kong.conf --nginx-conf custom_nginx.template
```

More details about customizing the Nginx configuration can be found **here**.

Play with Kong

There are lots of things that Kong can do for us.

- Kong as a proxy, passes requests to our backend services.
- Kong as middleware, can extend services with lots of functionality, such as transformation, rate-limit, etc.

- Kong as a resource manager, can manage users of services and protect services with an authentication layer.

In order to achieve these, we have to register an API, extend it with plugins, create a consumer, and authenticate with it. And this can be achieved by using Kong's internal RESTful Admin API. With this API, anything across Kong can be fully managed.

- 8001 is the default port on which the Admin API listens.
- 8444 is the default port for HTTPS traffic to the Admin API.

By issuing the request to `Admin API`, you'll get a response like below.

```
curl http://localhost:8001/

{
  "version": "0.12.1",
  "plugins": {
...... output truncated ......
  },
  "tagline": "Welcome to kong",
  "configuration": {
...... output truncated ......
  },
  "lua_version": "LuaJIT 2.1.0-beta3",
  "hostname": "Kong"
}
```

The response shows you the version of Kong, a list of enabled plugins, and several configured variables within Kong. From now on, we'll be using `Admin API` to manage APIs, configure plugins with API, and create a consumer for our APIs.

Add a new API

First, we need to make the Kong proxy specific requests to the service. In order to do that, we must tell Kong the specified rules of the request and how to retrieve the service. By requesting `Admin API` with the `/apis` endpoint, you can register and manage all ofthe API rules.

This table summarizes the verbs associated with the APIs:

Verb	Path	Description
POST	/apis	Creates an API

Verb	Path	Description
GET	/apis	List APIs
GET	/apis/{name or id}	Returns an existing API
PATCH	/apis/{name or id}	Updates an API
PUT	/apis/	Updates or creates an API
DELETE	/apis/{name or id}	Removes an existing API

- Adding APIs

```
POST /apis
Host: http://localhost:8001
 # Registering API must be specified with 'API Object'
```

Here is the API object:

Property	Description	Example	Required
name	Name of your API	my-API	*
hosts	Domain names point to your API	example1.com, example2.com	**
uris	URIs prefixes that point to your API	/my-path1, /my-path2	**
methods	HTTP methods that point to your API	GET, POST	**
upstream_url	Target URL point to your API server (target proxy)	**http://mockbin.com/**	*
strip_uri	strip matching prefix from the upstream URI @	[Default] True	
preserve_host	Request Host header is forwarded to upstream ^	[Default] False	
retries	Number of retries to execute upon failure to proxy	[Default] 5	

Property	Description	Example	Required
upstream_connect_timeout	Timeout for connection to upstream	[Default] 60000 (unit: ms)	
upstream_send_timeout	Timeout for sending a request to upstream	[Default] 60000 (unit: ms)	
upstream_read_timeout	Timeout for reading a response from upstream	[Default] 60000 (unit: ms)	
https_only	Serve an API through HTTPS only	[Default] False	
http_if_terminated	Allow X-Forwarded-Proto header on HTTPS only	[Default] False	

@: on `uris` match

^: on `hosts` match

**: At least one of `hosts`, `uris`, or `methods` should be specified.

Example: Adding our first API

As we created our `Cinema 3` microservice earlier, we will now register each microservice with `Creating API`. Before we register, let's test that our cinema microservice is running correctly.

```
curl http://localhost:8080/users

{
    "chris_rivers": {
        "id": "chris_rivers",
        "last_active": 1360031010,
        "name": "Chris Rivers"
    },
...... output truncated ......
```

It's running correctly! Let's register the `/users` API to Kong.

```
curl -i -X POST http://localhost:8001/apis/ \
 --data 'name=users' \
```

```
--data 'hosts=cinema.com' \
--data 'uris=/users' \
--data 'upstream_url=http://localhost:8080/users'
```

If successful with creating an API, the response should be:

```
{
  "created_at": 1517416945070,
  "strip_uri": true,
  "id": "06db17fc-15e1-4ac1-948b-6ec41355463f",
  "hosts": [
    "cinema.com"
  ],
  "name": "users",
  "http_if_terminated": false,
  "preserve_host": false,
  "upstream_url": "http:\/\/localhost:8080\/users",
  "uris": [
    "\/users"
  ],
  "upstream_connect_timeout": 60000,
  "upstream_send_timeout": 60000,
  "upstream_read_timeout": 60000,
  "retries": 5,
  "https_only": false
}
```

After creating an API, you can check your new registered API by issuing the request to Kong with `/users` URI.

```
curl -i -X GET http://localhost:8000/users \
  --header 'Host: cinema.com'

{
    "chris_rivers": {
        "id": "chris_rivers",
        "last_active": 1360031010,
        "name": "Chris Rivers"
    },
...... output truncated ......
```

You successfully registered your first API to Kong!

Using plugins with an API

Kong plugins can empower your service with lots of extensibility, such as authentication, security, traffic, Logging, etc. A full list of plugins can be shown **here**. By requesting `Admin API` with the `/plugins` endpoint, you can easily extend your API with Kong plugins.

This table summarize the verbs associated with the plugins:

Verb	Path	Description
POST	/apis/{name or id}/plugins/	Add Plugin to specific API
GET	/plugins/{plugin id}	Returns an specific Plugin
GET	/plugins/	List All Plugins
GET	/apis/{name or id}/plugins/	List Plugins of specific API
PATCH	/apis/{name or id}/plugins/{plugin id}	Updates Plugin configuration of specific API
PUT	/apis/{name or id}/plugins/	Updates or Add an Plugin to specific API
DELETE	/apis/{name or id}/plugins/{plugin id}	Removes Plugin of specific API
GET	/plugins/enabled	List All Enabled Plugins
GET	/plugins/schema/{plugin name}	Returns Plugin Schema

- Adding Plugins

Plugins can be added in several ways:

Rules	Endpoint	consumer_id
Every API and Consumer *	/plugins	x
Every API and a specific Consumer	/plugins	o
For every Consumer and a specific API	/apis/{name or id}/plugins	x
For a specific Consumer and API	/apis/{name or id}/plugins	o

*: Consumer will be addressed later in this chapter.

```
POST /apis/{name or id}/plugins
Host: http://localhost:8001
 # Adding plugin must be specified with 'Plugin Object'
```

The Plugin object:

Property	Description	Example	Required
name	Name of plugin	key-auth	o
consumer_id	ID of the consumer (**)	8729c655-517d-457e-8648-781d5809f713	
config.{property}	plugin specific config property	config.hide_credentials = True	**

**: If provided, it overrides the setting for only a specified consumer

Example: Limiting requests to the API

In the previous section, we registered `/user` API to Kong by using our `Cinema 3` microservice. Now we'll extend our API by adding a new plugin. The **Rate Limiting** plugin helps you easily limit requests to your API with the count of request per seconds, minutes, hours, days, months or years. It can limit by `Consumer`, `Credential` or `IP`.

In this example, we'll limit requests of our `/user` API by 5 times a minute.

Before we start, let's check how the basic response of our API request looks like:

```
curl -i -X GET http://localhost:8000/users \
  --header 'Host: cinema.com'

HTTP/1.1 200 OK
Content-Type: application/json
Content-Length: 880
Connection: keep-alive
Server: nginx/1.13.8
```

```
Date: Wed, 31 Jan 2018 16:49:22 GMT
X-Kong-Upstream-Latency: 3
X-Kong-Proxy-Latency: 10
Via: kong/0.12.1

...... output truncated ......
```

Let's add the `Rate Limiting` plugin to our API.

```
curl -X POST http://localhost:8001/apis/users/plugins \
    --data "name=rate-limiting" \
    --data "config.minute=5"
```

Kong will respond with *HTTP 201 Created* with the body of something like this:


```
{
  "created_at": 1517417022000,
  "config": {
    "hide_client_headers": false,
    "minute": 5,
...... output truncated ......
  },
  "id": "3e4c528b-37e7-4827-ae31-9dcc616e051c",
  "name": "rate-limiting",
  "api_id": "06db17fc-15e1-4ac1-948b-6ec41355463f",
  "enabled": true
}
```


To verify if the plugin registered to the API successfully:

```
curl -i -X GET http://localhost:8000/users \
  --header 'Host: cinema.com'

HTTP/1.1 200 OK
Content-Type: application/json
Content-Length: 880
Connection: keep-alive
X-RateLimit-Limit-minute: 5
X-RateLimit-Remaining-minute: 4
Server: nginx/1.13.8
Date: Wed, 31 Jan 2018 16:48:12 GMT
X-Kong-Upstream-Latency: 2
X-Kong-Proxy-Latency: 132
Via: kong/0.12.1

...... output truncated ......
```

As you can see in the header, `X-RateLimit-Limit-minute` and `X-RateLimit-Remaining-minute` has been added to the response. Issuing the same request will decrease the `X-RateLimit-Remaining-minute` till it gets to `0`.

```
curl -s -i -X GET http://localhost:8000/users \
  --header 'Host: cinema.com'

X-RateLimit-Remaining-minute: 1
...
X-RateLimit-Remaining-minute: 0
...

HTTP/1.1 429
Date: Wed, 31 Jan 2018 16:56:39 GMT
Content-Type: application/json; charset=utf-8
Transfer-Encoding: chunked
Connection: keep-alive
X-RateLimit-Limit-minute: 5
X-RateLimit-Remaining-minute: 0
Server: kong/0.12.1

{"message":"API rate limit exceeded"}
```

Finally, Kong responded with the message of "`API rate limit exceeded`".

We can find out through this example that it is really easy to extend API with plugins. In the next section, we'll add a consumer of an API and add an authentication plugin to protect our service with an authentication layer.

Creating consumers

After creating an API, configuring the third-parties that want to consume our API is needed, and those third-parties must be added to the database of Kong as consumers. A consumer can be associated with individuals using your API and can be used for tracking, access management, and more. By requesting `Admin API` with the `/consumers` endpoint, you can create and manage consumers for your API.

This table summarizes the verbs associated with the resource consumer:

Verb	Path	Description
GET	/consumers	List consumers
GET	/consumers/{username or id}	Returns an existing consumer
POST	/consumers/	Creates a new consumer
PATCH	/consumers/{username or id}	Updates an existing consumer
PUT	/consumers/	Updates or creates a consumer
DELETE	/consumers/{username or id}	Removes an existing consumer

- Adding Consumers

```
POST /consumers
Host: http://localhost:8001
 # Adding consumer must be specified with 'Consumer Object'
```

This is the consumer object:

Property	Description	Example	Required
username	Unique username of the consumer	Audience	**
consumer_id	Unique ID for the con- sumer	Audience- Kv4qck341	**

**: Either `username` or `consumer_id` must be provided.

Example: Protect APIs with a consumer & authentication layer

Let's assume that there are some third-parties who want to consume our APIs. And it is really necessary to authenticate each of them whether they can access the API or not. In this situation, managing all third-parties and controlling access to each API might be really hard. To solve this problem, with Kong you can bind each of the third-parties as a consumer, and control access of the APIs with authentication on the basis of the consumer.

The first step to create a consumer is to POST a new resource to the collection Consumers. The following command will be used to create a new Consumer called 'Audience':

```
curl -X POST http://localhost:8001/consumers \
    --data "username=Audience"
```

Kong will return a *HTTP 201 Created* in case the operation was successful, with this JSON object as a response:

```
{
  "created_at": 1517421007000,
  "username": "Audience",
  "id": "515e7c01-36f1-4448-b726-b67f3a6a5cdc"
}
```

It is possible to check if the Consumer was created by using a GET operation to retrieve the collection of Consumers:

```
curl -X GET http://localhost:8001/consumers/

{
  "total": 1,
  "data": [
    {
      "created_at": 1517421007000,
      "username": "Audience",
      "id": "515e7c01-36f1-4448-b726-b67f3a6a5cdc"
    }
  ]
}
```

Now that the consumer has been created, we'll protect our API by creating an authentication layer. The **Key Authentication** plugin helps you to secure your API from unauthorized use. After adding this plugin, only requests with the correct API key will be proxied and all other requests will be rejected.

To begin, add the key authentication plugin to your API.

```
curl -i -X POST \
  --url http://localhost:8001/apis/users/plugins/ \
  --data 'name=key-auth'
```

With a successful **HTTP 201 Created** response, a body will be similar to below.

```
{
  "created_at": 1517421772000,
  "config": {
    "key_in_body": false,
```

```
      "run_on_preflight": true,
      "anonymous": "",
      "hide_credentials": false,
      "key_names": [
        "apikey"
      ]
    },
    "id": "34c1df34-ae4b-41c7-b92f-1b5c6e404e7f",
    "name": "key-auth",
    "api_id": "06db17fc-15e1-4ac1-948b-6ec41355463f",
    "enabled": true
  }
```

As configured, verify the plugin by issuing the command below.

```
curl -i -X GET http://localhost:8000/users \
  --header 'Host: cinema.com'
```

If your response is `401 Unauthorized`, don't panic. It's a deserved result, because we didn't specify any `apikey` header or parameter.

```
HTTP/1.1 401 Unauthorized
...

{
  "message": "No API key found in request"
}
```

Now, back to our consumer `Audience`. Issue the command below to add an API key for authentication purposes.

```
curl -i -X POST http://localhost:8001/consumers/Audience/key-
auth/ \
  --data 'key=backStopMedia'

{
  "id": "452146e7-a1f1-4cb7-afb6-fa7a2d0d5ad0",
  "created_at": 1517422375000,
  "key": "backStopMedia",
  "consumer_id": "515e7c01-36f1-4448-b726-b67f3a6a5cdc"
}
```

Finally, with our created API Key, make a request to our API with the header of `apikey`.

```
curl -i -X GET http://localhost:8000/users \
  --header 'Host: cinema.com' \
  --header "apikey: backStopMedia"

{
    "chris_rivers": {
        "id": "chris_rivers",
        "last_active": 1360031010,
        "name": "Chris Rivers"
    },
...... output truncated ......
```

You've succeeded in protecting your API with a consumer and authentication layer!

Sizing up Kong

Let's assume that your service got famous, and requests are increasing explosively so much that your server resources can't handle it. Now it's time for you to scale your resources, by adding more servers.

And with scaling servers, what would you have to do for proxying requests to hit each server equally? In this situation, load balancing might be the right answer. By putting the load balancer in front of your servers, it will take care of your traffic in a balanced manner.

By using the load balancer, what would happen if one of your servers goes down, and you don't know which one it is? It would be a total disaster. To prevent this situation and to achieve high availability, you will have to monitor each server status whether it is healthy or not.

In this chapter, we'll learn how to handle a lot of traffic with the load balancer, and how to route this traffic only to health services.
We'll also cover how to deal with a Kong cluster, which is a scaled out multiple instance of Kong.

Load Balancing

Kong, which is in front of many services, can work as a load balancer. By the position of where Kong is placed, it can unify the control point of services to manage traffic.

With this unified control point, several things become available:

- Route client requests across all servers.

- Traffic requests with monitoring utilization, by ensuring no single server is overloaded.

To make Kong work as a load balancer, we need to configure Kong.
Kong is capable of load balancing in several ways:
1) DNS-based load balancing

This method doesn't require Kong to configure any settings. In DNS-Based load balancing, the registration of upstream services is done with a DNS service provider, and Kong only receives results from the DNS server.

A records: Contains one or more IP addresses.

No weight information, since all entries are treated with equal weight. (Straight round-robin)

Type	Name	Value	TTL
A	user.backend.com	123.123.123.xxx	3h
A	user.backend.com	123.221.221.xxx	3h

SRV records: Contains weight and port information for all of its IP addresses.

Each entry will be treated with own weight. (Weighted round-robin)

Type	Service.Protocol.Host	Priority	Weight	Port	Target	TTL
SRV	user._tcp.backend.com	5	0	5269	user.backend.com	3600

For more about DNS-based load balancing, see **here**

2) Dynamic ring-balancer based load balancing

By using the ring-balancer method, all of the services will be managed by Kong as the service registry. `upstream` and `target` entities are used for configuring the ring-balancer.

upstream: 'Virtual hostname,' which will be used in an API `upstream_url` field.

ex) upstream named `user.backend.service`would get all requests from an API with `upstream_url=http://user.backend.service/some/path`.

target: IP or hostname with a port that directs service. With a weight value provided, the relative load gets it.
ex) `123.123.123.xxx:80`

Load Balancing Algorithms
Dynamic ring-balancer uses weighted-round-robin as a default. As an alternative, hash-based algorithms can be used. There are several options for which target to hash on.

```
    -    `Consumer`: use consumer id as a hash input.
(fallback on credential id)
    -    `IP`: use remote (originating) IP address as hash
input
    -    `Header`: use a specified header (specify with
`hash_on_header` or `hash_fallback_header`)
```

In this section, we'll only address dynamic ring-balancer, which Kong is the subject of.

Upstream

As mentioned before, `upstream` is the 'Virtual hostname' for a set of API's `upstream_urls`. Each `target` is registered to upstream, and the upstream load balance traffics over these targets with its own ring-balancer. By requesting `Admin API` with the `/upstreams` endpoint, you can manage upstream and load balancing policy for your API.

This table summarize the verbs associated with the resource Upstream:

Verb	Path	Description
POST	/upstreams/	Creates a new upstream
GET	/upstreams/{name or id}	Returns an existing upstream
GET	/upstreams/	List upstreams
PATCH	/upstreams/{name or id}	Updates an existing upstream
PUT	/upstreams/	Updates or creates a upstream
DELETE	/upstreams/{name or id}	Removes an existing upstream

- Adding upstream

```
POST /upstreams
Host: http://localhost:8001
 # Adding upstream must be specified with 'Upstream Object'
```

The Upstream object:

Property	Description	Example	Required
name	Alias for upstream_url (hostname)	service.v1.xyz	o
slots	Number of slots in the loadbalancer algorithm	[Defaults] 1000 (10-65536)	
hash_on	Hashing input: none, consumer, ip, or header	[Defaults] None	
hash_fallback	Fallback for Hashing input *	[Defaults] None	
hash_on_header	Header name for hash input **		*
hash_fallback_header	Header name for fallback hash input **		*
healthchecks	Health check fields		

: eg. Missing Header, no Consumer identified

*

: only on 'hash_on' set header

Target

Each `target` is registered with a `weight` value, which is the basis for determining relative load traffic. By requesting `Admin API` with the `/upstreams/{name or id}/targets` endpoint, you can manage targets with each weight for LB over the services endpoint.

This table summarizes the verbs associated with the resource Target:

Verb	Path	Description
POST	/upstreams/{name or id}/targets	Creates a new target to upstream
GET	/upstreams/{name or id}/targets *	Returns active list of targets to upstream
GET	/upstreams/{name or id}/targets/all *	List all targets of upstreams

Verb	Path	Description
DELETE	/upstreams/{name or id}/ targets/{target or id}	Removes a target from up-stream

*: Change in the Kong 0.12.0 release.

- Adding upstream's target

```
POST /upstreams/{name or id}/targets
Host: http://localhost:8001
```

Property	Description	Example	Required
target	Address (IP or hostname) and Port	localhost:8080 (de-fault 8000 port)	O
weight	weight of target for load balancing *	[Defaults] 100 (0-1000)	

*: If the host resolves the SRV record, override the value with a DNS record.

Example: Load balance our service

Let's assume that our `cinema`'s `users` service got famous and by increased traffic, our service can't handle requests. In this case, to solve this problem, we'll have to scale our service. In this example, we'll scale our service, handling it with Kong 'ring-based' load balancer.

Before we start this example, we'll use another branch `scale` to only focus on scaling our services.

```
# from your cinema working directory
git checkout scale
```

The first step is scaling our service. Here, as we've created our service with docker-compose, we'll scale out our `user` service with the `--scale` option:

```
# [on scale branch] from your cinema working directory
docker-compose up --scale users=2

...... output truncated ......
users_2      |  * Running on http://0.0.0.0:5000/ (Press CTRL
```

```
+C to quit)
users_2      |  * Restarting with stat
...... output truncated ......
users_1      |  * Running on http://0.0.0.0:5000/ (Press CTRL
+C to quit)
users_1      |  * Restarting with stat

 # From this command, you can monitor each services with
incoming requests in real time.
```

To check that our scaled services are correctly running, issue the below command.

```
docker-compose ps

       Name                Command       State
Ports
--------------------------------------------------------------------
cinema3_bookings_1    python app.py
Up
cinema3_movies_1      python app.py
Up
cinema3_showtimes_1   python app.py
Up
cinema3_users_1       python app.py   Up      0.0.0.0:5000-
>5000/tcp
cinema3_users_2       python app.py   Up      0.0.0.0:5001-
>5000/tcp
```

We can see that the `users_1` and `users_2` service is running on 5000, 5001 port. To check that the service is running correctly, issue commands to each port.

```
curl -X GET http://localhost:5000

{"total": 1,
...... output truncated ......

curl -X GET http://localhost:5001

{"total": 1,
...... output truncated ......
```

Now that we've checked that our scaled services are working correctly, let's create `upstream` with the name `users.service` for Kong to load balance our service.

```
curl -i -X POST http://localhost:8001/upstreams \
  --data 'name=users.service'

{
  "created_at": 1517686540804,
  "hash_on": "none",
  "id": "cb2947e0-1b4f-4688-a648-355172226b86",
  "healthchecks": {
...... output truncated ......
  },
  "name": "users.service",
  "hash_fallback": "none",
  "slots": 100
}
```

Our upstream has been created sucessfully. Now it's time to add our `targets` to `upstream`.

```
curl -i -X POST http://localhost:8001/upstreams/
users.service/targets \
  --data 'target=localhost:5000'

{
  "created_at": 1517686986852,
  "weight": 100,
  "upstream_id": "cb2947e0-1b4f-4688-a648-355172226b86",
  "target": "localhost:5000",
  "id": "e64a6fc5-e2ee-4381-81d6-7458842c0e1d"
}

curl -i -X POST http://localhost:8001/upstreams/
users.service/targets \
  --data 'target=localhost:5001'

{
  "created_at": 1517687652712,
  "weight": 100,
  "upstream_id": "cb2947e0-1b4f-4688-a648-355172226b86",
  "target": "localhost:5001",
  "id": "07716e92-58b8-460c-acab-60cb25e51eb1"
}
```

Our targets have been added to upstream successfully, so now we'll configure our `users` API's upstream_url with new `users.service`.

```
curl -X PATCH http://localhost:8001/apis/users \
  --data 'upstream_url=http://users.service'
```

```
{
...... output truncated ......
  "upstream_url": "http:\/\/users.service"
}
```

It's time to verify our upstream to see if it is working as a load balancer correctly.

```
curl -i -X GET http://localhost:8000/users \
  --header 'Host: cinema.com' \

users_2       | 172.18.0.1 - - [03/Feb/2018 20:20:10] "GET /
HTTP/1.1" 200 -
users_1       | 172.18.0.1 - - [03/Feb/2018 20:20:12] "GET /
HTTP/1.1" 200 -
users_2       | 172.18.0.1 - - [03/Feb/2018 20:20:13] "GET /
HTTP/1.1" 200 -
users_1       | 172.18.0.1 - - [03/Feb/2018 20:20:13] "GET /
HTTP/1.1" 200 -
...... output truncated ......
```

As each targets weight has been configured to default 100, it will balance requests equal to each targets.
You've just created `upstream` and `targets`, and successfully load balanced with it!

Health check your API

We've just created a load balancer with Kong. Now it's time to create a health checker to decide whether it is safe to transfer traffic to each service. By monitoring each service to see if it is alive or not, we can achieve high availability with our service.

There are two types of health checks that can be done with Kong.

- Active HC: Periodically request the specific HTTP endpoint, and check that the service is healthy with that response.
  Automatically enable and disable targets with the load balancer.
- Passive HC (Circuit Breaker): Monitor the ongoing traffic to each service, and determine a healthy response of traffic. To enable the target, Admin API is used to notify the health status of the target.

By the results of the health check, load balancers are able to keep traffic stable without any errors.

- Adding Health Check

```
POST /upstreams
Host: http://localhost:8001
 # Adding Health check must be specified with 'Upstream
Object'
```

The Active Healthcheck Properties (prefix - healthcheck):

Property	Description	Default
active.timeout	Socket timeout for HTTP Request	1
active.concurrency	Number of targets to check concurrently.	10
active.http_path	Path to GET HTTP request for active HC probe	"/"
active.healthy.interval	Interval between active HC for healthy targets *	0 (disabled)
active.healthy.http_statuses	HTTP statuses to consider a healthy	200,302
active.healthy.successes	Success count to consider a healthy target. ‡	ex) 5
active.unhealthy.interval	Interval between active HC for unhealthy targets. *	0 (disabled)
active.unhealthy.http_statuses	HTTP Failure count to consider a target unhealthy. **	429,404,5xx
active.unhealthy.tcp_failures	Number of TCP failures to consider a target unhealthy.	ex) 5
active.unhealthy.timeouts	Number of timeouts to consider a target unhealthy.	ex) 5
active.unhealthy.http_failures	HTTP Failure count to consider a target unhealthy. **	ex) 5

The Active Healthcheck Properties (prefix - healthcheck):

Property	Description	Example
passive.healthy.http_statuses	HTTP statuses to consider healthy	2xx, 3xx

Property	Description	Example
passive.healthy.successes	Success count to consider a target healthy **	ex) 5
passive.unhealthy.http_statuses	HTTP statuses to consider an unhealthy	429,500,503
passive.unhealthy.tcp_failures	TCP failure count to consider a target unhealthy.	ex) 5
passive.unhealthy.timeouts	Number of timeouts to consider a target unhealthy.	ex) 5
passive.unhealthy.http_failures	HTTP Failure count to consider a target unhealthy. **	ex) 5

: A value of zero indicates that active probes for healthy targets should not be performed.

*

: As defined in its http_statuses.

Example: Health Check our service

From the load balancer example, we've created the `users.service` upstream. Now we'll add a `active` health check to the same upstream.

```
curl -i -X PATCH http://localhost:8001/upstreams/
users.service \
  --data 'healthchecks.active.http_path=/' \
  --data 'healthchecks.active.healthy.interval=5' \
  --data 'healthchecks.active.healthy.successes=3' \
  --data 'healthchecks.active.unhealthy.interval=5' \
  --data 'healthchecks.active.unhealthy.timeouts=3' \
  --data 'healthchecks.active.unhealthy.tcp_failures=3' \
  --data 'healthchecks.active.unhealthy.http_failures=3'
```

```
{
  "created_at": 1517686540804,
  "hash_on": "none",
  "id": "cb2947e0-1b4f-4688-a648-355172226b86",
  "healthchecks": {
    "active": {
      "unhealthy": {
        "http_statuses": [429,404,500,501,502,503,504,505],
        "interval": 5,
        "timeouts": 3,
```

```
        "http_failures": 3,
        "tcp_failures": 3
      },
      "http_path": "\/",
      "healthy": {
        "successes": 3,
        "interval": 5,
        "http_statuses": [200,302]
      },
      "timeout": 1,
      "concurrency": 10
    },
    "passive": {
...... output truncated ......
    }
  },
  "name": "users.service",
  "hash_fallback": "none",
  "slots": 100
}
```

By this, our upstream will probe our targets in 5 second intervals, and if it succeeds or fails five times in a row, it will report the target as healthy or unhealthy. Now we'll try to scale in our `users` service to 0, to check what happens to upstream if no service is running.

```
 # [on scale branch] from your cinema working directory
docker-compose up -d --scale users=0
tail -f /usr/local/kong/logs/error.log

...... output truncated ......
... [warn] ... [healthcheck] (users.service) unhealthy TCP
increment (1/3) for 127.0.0.1:5000, context: ngx.timer,
client: ...
... [warn] ... [healthcheck] (users.service) unhealthy TCP
increment (1/3) for 127.0.0.1:5001, context: ngx.timer,
client: ...
... [warn] ... [healthcheck] (users.service) unhealthy TCP
increment (2/3) for 127.0.0.1:5000, context: ngx.timer,
client: ...
... [warn] ... [healthcheck] (users.service) unhealthy TCP
increment (2/3) for 127.0.0.1:5001, context: ngx.timer,
client: ...
... [warn] ... [healthcheck] (users.service) unhealthy TCP
increment (3/3) for 127.0.0.1:5000, context: ngx.timer,
client: ...
... [warn] 90#0: *7467 [lua] healthcheck.lua:957: log():
[healthcheck] (users.service) unhealthy TCP increment (3/3)
```

```
for 127.0.0.1:5001, context: ngx.timer, client: ...
...... output truncated ......
```

The Kong log will show you errors with unhealthy TCP request to targets. If it reaches the unhealthy limit, Kong will return **503 Service Temporarily Unavailable** with the unreachable target.

```
$ curl -i -X GET http://localhost:8000/users \
  --header 'Host: cinema.com'

HTTP/1.1 503 Service Temporarily Unavailable
...... output truncated ......
Server: kong/0.12.1

{"message":"failure to get a peer from the ring-balancer"}
```

Now, we'll re-add our `users` service to 1 to check if upstream is working correctly.

```
 # [on scale branch] from your cinema working directory
docker-compose up --scale users=1
tail -f /usr/local/kong/logs/error.log

...... output truncated ......
... [warn] ... [healthcheck] (users.service) healthy SUCCESS
increment (1/3) for 127.0.0.1:5000, context: ngx.timer
... [warn] ... [healthcheck] (users.service) healthy SUCCESS
increment (2/3) for 127.0.0.1:5000, context: ngx.timer
... [warn] 87#0: *9187 [lua] healthcheck.lua:957: log():
[healthcheck] (users.service) healthy SUCCESS increment
(3/3) for 127.0.0.1:5000, context: ngx.timer
...... output truncated ......
```

Since our target has been checked healthy, a request to the `Users` API will be proxied to healthy targets.

```
$ curl -i -X GET http://localhost:8000/users \
  --header 'Host: cinema.com'

HTTP/1.1 200 OK
...... output truncated ......
Via: kong/0.12.1

{
    "subresource_uris": {
        "bookings": "/users/<username>/bookings",
        "suggested": "/users/<username>/suggested",
```

```
            "user": "/users/<username>",
            "users": "/users"
        },
        "uri": "/"
    }
```

You've just added `Health Check` to `upstream`, and tested target's status from `unhealthy` to `healthy`!

Clustering

To handle much more traffic requests to Kong, you need more instances. Kong nodes pointing to the same database and sharing the same configurations are called as a Kong cluster. To make a Kong cluster work, you need to not only create lots of Kong instances, but you also need a **load balancer** in front of it to distribute traffic to each node.

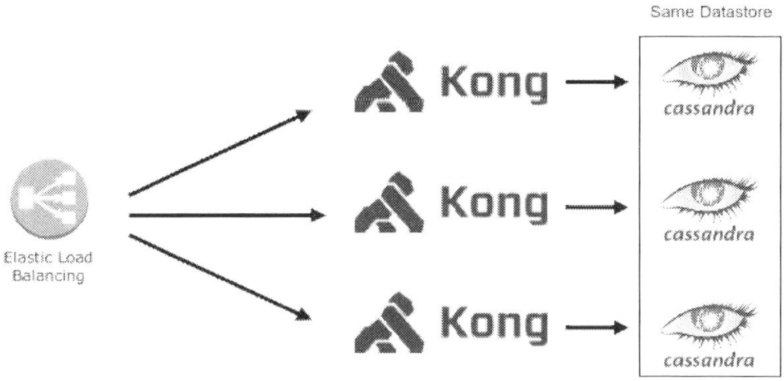

CACHING

For Kong to respond faster, Kong avoids database connections when proxying requests, and caches the contents of the database in memory. Cached data are APIs, Consumers, Plugins, Credentials, etc. Since each Kong node has its own cached data, any changes applied through Admin API needs to be propagated to others.

- Single Kong node Cluster: any changes applied through the Admin API will be applied instantly.
- Multi Kong node Cluster: any changes to other nodes will be fetched by each node through periodic background synchronized jobs.

`db_update_frequency`: A period of lookup for any update in datastore (default: 5 sec).

By this configuration, each node will poll the database and keep the cached content updated. As a consequence, a Kong cluster becomes eventually consistent.

A more detailed configuration of caching can be found **here**.

Summary

Through the extensive details of multiple examples in this chapter, you have seen Kong in action. In the next chapter you will see how to extend Kong.

Extending Kong 6

Kong has a bunch of features out of the box, including different authentication strategies, request/response transformations, traffic control, logging systems support and more (the full list of available plugins is available in the **documentation**, including Kong enterprise plugins). But it is also very flexible in adding custom plugins - **Lua language**, **OpenResty** platform, **Lapis framework** and Kong DAO factory allows you to build a plugin of any complexity, add new entrypoints to Kong admin, work with a databases, etc. The power of the plugin system is limited only by system resources and a developer's imagination.

In this chapter we'll cover how to create a custom plugin from scratch, how to organize modules, and how to test and install it. And we'll start with the latest versions, since it's convenient to see how the plugin works during development.

To create a Kong plugin you need a running Kong instance. A **local Kong installation** is the easiest way to get started, and for the examples covered in this chapter we assume you have a default Kong setup without any plugins configured. Of course it's possible to use a Docker container for our cinema microservices example, although it gets more complicated installing and testing the plugin. In the real world, building a Kong plugin in Docker is only required for unsupported systems (e.g. Windows).

So, let's start with plugin installation.

All of the code for the sample project in this book can be found **here**.

Installing custom plugins

It's possible to install a plugin from any source, but the fastest and easiest way - is to use **luarocks**. It's a package manager for Lua and Kong's official installation package includes it already. So, just search for the desired plugin either on the website or locally with the `luarocks search` command and run the `install`:

```
luarocks install <your-plugin>
```

Where `<your-plugin>`-is the name of the rock file, usually located at `luarocks.org`, but its possible to use a direct URL to it.

It will install the latest version of the plugin to the rocks tree-a path in your system where Lua is able to load modules. You can see detailed information about the plugin (and any Lua library) with the `show` command:

```
luarocks show <your-plugin>
```

Besides the description, it will show the physical path of installed modules.

It's possible to install any version (in case the latest doesn't work for you or it is broken):

```
luarocks install <your-plugin> <version>
```

Manually

While developing a plugin locally, you can't install it from luarocks-it simply doesn't exist there. For that there are a couple more methods to install a plugin:

1. Modify the `lua_package_path` configuration option the way it will point to your plugin path.
2. With the `luarocks make` command.
3. With Docker.

Before using any of them, you need to upload a plugin to the target machine (can skip this step for local development). It's totally up to you how to deliver the plugin code to the server, either in the archive or with git-all will work.

To change the Kong `lua_package_path` configuration, you can either edit a `lua_package_path` variable in `nginx-kong.conf` or set the environment variable KONG_LUA_PACKAGE_PATH. The value of this variable is in a standard Lua path form, with `;` as a separator. `;;` refers to original search path, so make sure not to remove it. The full description of `lua_package_path` is available at **Lua nginx module documenta-**

tion. So, if you have the plugin in /kong/plugins/your-plugin directory, your lua_package_path may look like this:

```
lua_package_path ./?.lua;./?/init.lua;/kong/plugins/your-
plugin/?.lua;;
```

With this method you won't pollute the Lua rocks tree and you will just need to restart a server if the plugin code changes.

To use a luarocks make command, you need to have a source code of the plugin somewhere at your machine and run that command:

```
cd <path to your plugin>
luarocks make
```

It will install the plugin to kong/plugins/<your-plugin> in your rocks tree path. After each code change-luarocks make should be run again with Kong restart to apply changes.

To develop plugins in Docker, you need a Kong image, and you must load a volume with your plugin code into a directory, where Kong will find it (may vary, depending on your Kong installation), and reload Kong server after each code change. Don't worry if it sounds complex, we will have a detailed example installing a custom plugin into our cinema Docker Compose configuration.

Loading plugins

Once your plugin is installed, you need to load it. And again, you have a couple of ways to do so: via the custom_plugins configuration attribute in nginx-kong.conf or with the KONG_CUSTOM_PLUGINS environment variable. Multiple plugins should be separated by commas:

```
custom_plugins = your-plugin1,your-plugin2
```

After a Kong reload, you will be able to use your plugin. In the cluster you need to repeat the installation process on each node. To verify that the plugin was installed correctly, hit the kong API and check the plugins field under `configuration. Assuming Kong API is listening at 8001 port locally (Python is used for pretty print here):

```
curl -XGET "localhost:8001" | python -mjson.tool
```

```
{
    "configuration": {
      ...
        "plugins": {
          "acl": true,
          "aws-lambda": true,
          ...
          "your-plugin": true,
          ...
```

Once loading is done, we are ready to apply the plugin to APIs and consumers.

Building your own plugin

Integrating with a third-party service is a typical task developers solve with Kong. Since each service has its own API, business logic and purpose, writing a custom plugin is a good way to make it work. It's impossible to write a universal plugin, but we will make an attempt to create a general purpose notification plugin, which may be used for notificating different services when specified Kong endpoints are hit.

Kong plugins are written in the Lua language, but if you're not familiar with it, its not a problem. Lua is a scripting language, and it supports different programming paradigms as Kong provides you with a clean, understandable interface to work with it, so even without knowledge you can develop it fast.

So, our plugin will send an asynchronous request to the external server on each request to the Kong API it applied to. Optionally, it will send a notification for specified consumers. It should allow you to configure a target server and the data which you send. Furthermore, it will save the history of requests into the database. We will cover: the Kong plugin interface, how to create a database migration, how to query a Kong database, and how to send a separate request from the Kong plugin (we will write tests for that).

Kong has a beautiful and very detailed **documentation** about how to create a plugin. Let's start with a basic code structure. Kong plugins live in the `kong/plugins` namespace. The kong-notification-plugin directory itself can be anywhere, because it's the root directory of the plugin. Also, **here is a link** to the final plugin source code, and the path:

```
kong-notification-plugin
|       └── kong
```

```
|               └── plugins
|                   └── notification
```

Okay, now we can get started:

```
mkdir kong-notification-plugin
cd kong-notification-plugin
mkdir -p kong/plugins
touch kong/plugins/handler.lua
touch kong/plugins/schema.lua
```

Here we created a basic plugin structure that now looks like this:

```
kong-notification-plugin/kong/plugins/notification
├── handler.lua
└── schema.lua
```

Now, we can install it to our cinema Docker Compose configuration. First, we need to load a volume to both `kong-migration` and `kong` services:

```
services:
  ...
  kong-migration:
    build: ./kong
    volumes:
      - ../kong-notification-plugin/kong/plugins/
notification:/usr/local/share/lua/5.1/kong/plugins/
notification:ro
  ...
  kong:
    build: ./kong
    volumes:
      - ../kong-notification-plugin/kong/plugins/
notification:/usr/local/share/lua/5.1/kong/plugins/
notification:ro
```

This setup expects you to have `kong-notification-plugin` and `kong-book-example` directories at the same level in your directory structure. The container path `/usr/local/share/lua/5.1/kong/plugins/notification` is special-it will allow Kong to find your plugin. Using a different path and changing the KONG_LUA_PACKAGE_PATH environment variable will not work, and your plugin migrations will not be loaded (there are a couple issues regarding this problem at Github at the moment of writing this book). The last step is to load plugin to Kong-for that simply add the `KONG_CUSTOM_PLUGINS` environment variable:

```
services:
  ...
  kong-migration:
    ...
    environment:
      ...
      - KONG_CUSTOM_PLUGINS=notification
  kong:
    ...
    environment:
      ...
      - KONG_CUSTOM_PLUGINS=notification
```

That's it. Running `docker-compose up -d` will run the container with the plugin enabled. After a code change we need to reload a server. One way is to run `docker-compose stop` and `docker-compose up`, but there is a faster way-`exec` into running a Kong container and reload Kong directly:

```
docker exec -it 545018ec05dd sh
/ # kong reload
Kong reloaded
```

where `545018ec05dd` is the Kong container id (you will have a different id), which you can easily fit on one line:

```
docker ps | grep "kongbookexample_kong" | head -1 | cut -d'
' -f1
545018ec05dd
```

But notice, a Kong reload will not run any migrations we will add in the future. We still need to run a `kong-migration` container to do that.

If you develop your own plugin and don't use Docker, we recommend running the Kong server locally with a modified `lua_package_path` variable, which will include a path to your plugin root directory. That way you will be able to test the plugin immediately after the code change and the Kong reload.

Plugin configuration

Plugin configuration is a way to change how a plugin behaves for different APIs or consumers. In the datastore, all plugins are saved in the `plugins` table with `name`, `api_id`, `consumer_id` and its `config`, which is a JSON field received by the Kong API when the plugin is added.

We want you to be able to send notifications to different servers and by different methods for different APIs and consumers. So, the notification plugin will have two configuration parameters: `url` where the request will be sent and the `method`. We will also have `timeout` and `keepalive`, which will be used later for the connection configuration.

In the code, the plugin configuration is defined in the `schema.lua` file, which should return a Lua table:

- `no_consumer` - allows you to apply a plugin to specific consumers if `false` (a default)
- `fields` - actual configuration table
- `self_check` - custom validation functions

```
-- schema.lua
return {
  fields = {
    url = {type = "string", required = true},
    method = {type = "string", required = true},
    timeout = {default = 10000, type = "number"},
    keepalive = {default = 60000, type = "number"}
  }
}
```

In the snippet above we added two required fields: `url` and `method`, both of `string` type and two optional with defaults: `timeout` and `keealive`. It's possible to set a default value, and make a configuration field immutable (not allowed to change after set the first time) or unique.

Having such a confuguration schema will not allow a client to apply an invalid one, like missing fields or wrong values. It's also a good idea to add some validations, like methods allowed, and validating a URL by the regex:

```
-- schema.lua
...
    url = {type = "string", required = true,
regex="^((http[s]?):\/)?\/?([^:\/\s]+)((\/\w+)*\/)([\w\-\.]+
[^#?\s]+)(.*)?(#[\w\-]+)?$"},
```

```
    method = {type = "string", required = true, enum =
{"GET", "POST", "PUT"}}
...
```

Fortunately, Kong already has a `url` type defined, so using the regex validator is not needed, so just change a type to URL:

```
-- schema.lua
    url = {type = "url", required = true},
```

Kong supports a custom validator within the `func` parameter. It receives a value and should return either `true` or `false, <error message>`, where `<error message>` is your validation error. The difference between `func` and `self_check` is that the latest is applied for the whole schema after all other validations are passed, so it's possible to validate rules applied to multiple configuration fields (e.g. a whitelist or blacklist set).

Kong supports many other configuration types, including complex (`table`, `array`, etc). For example, if you need a nested configuration, you can add a `schema` parameter to validate nested fields:

```
-- schema.lua
let nested_schema = {fields = {...}}

...
  nested_field = {type = "table", schema=nested_schema}
...
```

The full list of available types and validators is available in the **Kong documentation**. That's it with configuration for now, since we have to implement the logic of the plugin.

The core of the plugin

The execution process consists of several phases, and there are some limitations about what is possible in each phase and callback. The table below displays the Lua Nginx module directives and appropriate Kong callbacks in execution order:

Order	Lua nginx module function	Kong callback	Phase
1	init_worker_by_lua	:init_worker()	initialization

Order	Lua nginx module function	Kong callback	Phase
2	ssl_certificate_by_lua	:certificate()	rewrite/access
3	rewrite_by_lua	:rewrite()	rewrite/access
4	access_by_lua	:access()	rewrite/access
5	header_filter_by_lua	:header_filter()	content
6	body_filter_by_lua	:body_filter()	content
7	log_by_lua	:log()	log

The complete description of execution phases and Lua Nginx module directives is available at the **github repository**.

For the notification plugin we will implement an `:access()` callback, since it gets executed for each request before it's being proxied to the upstream. Kong provides a `base_plugin` module that is convenient to use (but not required) to log each hit of the callback of our plugin:

```
-- handler.lua
local BasePlugin = require "kong.plugins.base_plugin" --
import Kong base plugin
local NotificationHandler = BasePlugin:extend() -- inherit
from Kong base plugin

function NotificationHandler:new()
  NotificationHandler.super.new(self, "notification") --
call super module function with a plugin name (used for
logging)
end

function NotificationHandler:access(config) -- implement
access() callback
  NotificationHandler.super.access(self)
  -- Custom logic goes here
end

return NotificationHandler
```

Inheriting from the Kong base plugin allows you to log each callback call with a given plugin name. Here is an example for the `access()` callback:

```
-- kong/plugins/base_plugin.lua
function BasePlugin:new(name)
```

```
  self._name = name
end

...

function BasePlugin:access()
  ngx_log(DEBUG, "executing plugin \"", self._name, "\":
access")
end
```

When we call a function like `NotificationHandler.super.access(self)`, the code from the super module will be executed and a new DEBUG level log entry with the message `executing plugin "notification": access` will be added.

It's possible to not inherit from the `base_plugin`, but instead inherit from the `Object`:

```
-- handler.lua
local Object = require "kong.vendor.classic"
local NotificationHandler = Object:extend()

function NotificationHandler:access(config) -- implement
access() callback
  -- Custom logic goes here
end

return NotificationHandler
```

In this case there is no need to set a name or call super functions, and of course nothing will be logged under the hood.

So, the `access` callback receives a single parameter, `config`, which is a table described in `schema.lua`. It is the config for the exact `api` and `consumer`, stored in the `config` column of the `plugins` table in the datastore. The idea is to send an asynchronous request to the `config.url` with the method `config.method`. The algorithm is described next.

Notification plugin handler logic

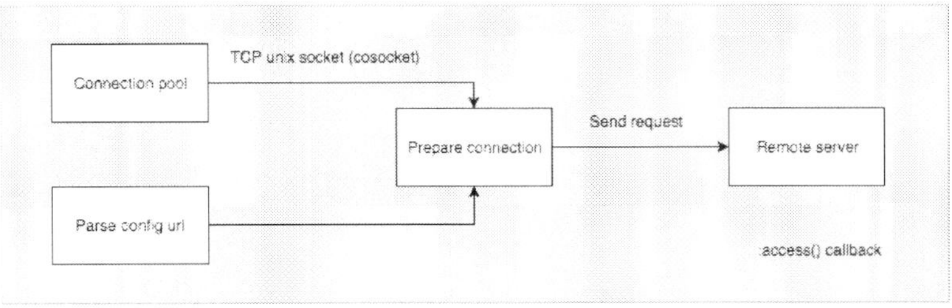

The first step is to parse a URL and get the protocol, domain, port, and path. For that task we can use a `socket.url` module included in Kong dependencies:

```
-- handler.lua
local socket_url = require "socket.url"

local function parse_url(url)
  local parsed_url = socket_url.parse(url)
  if not parsed_url.port then
    if parsed_url.scheme == "http" then
      parsed_url.port = 80
    elseif parsed_url.scheme == "https" then
      parsed_url.port = 443
    end
  end
  if not parsed_url.path then
    parsed_url.path = "/"
  end
  return parsed_url
end
```

To be able to send an external HTTP request, we need a kind of HTTP client, but Kong already has tools (actually it's a Lua nginx module) for sending requests with UDP and TCP protocols:

- `ngx.socket.tcp` for TCP connections
- `ngx.socket.udp` for UDP connections

Create a socket and connect it to the remote server. Also, it's a good idea to add logging in case of a failed connection:

```
--handler.lua
...
```

```
function NotificationHandler:access(config)
  NotificationHandler.super.access(self)

  local parsed_url = parse_url(config.url)
  local host = parsed_url.host
  local port = tonumber(parsed_url.port)

  local sock = ngx.socket.tcp() -- Creates and returns a TCP
or stream-oriented unix domain socket object
  sock:settimeout(config.timeout) -- Set the timeout value
in milliseconds for subsequent socket operations
  ok, err = sock:connect(host, port)
  if not ok then
    ngx.log(ngx.ERR, "[notification-log] failed to connect
to " .. host .. ":" .. tostring(port) .. ": ", err)
    return
  end
end
```

Notice the `config` variable is the table with keys, defined in the `schema.lua` module of the plugin, and values are set for the request API and the consumer.

In case the remote server uses the `https` protocol we need to add the **SSL handshake**:

```
--handler.lua
...
  if parsed_url.scheme == "https" then
    local _, err = sock:sslhandshake(true, host, false)
    if err then
      ngx.log(ngx.ERR, "[notification-log] failed to do SSL
handshake with " .. host .. ":" .. tostring(port) .. ": ",
err)
    end
  end
```

Before sending a message we need to create it:

```
--handler.lua
local cjson = require "cjson"

local string_format = string.format
local cjson_encode = cjson.encode

local function get_message(config, parsed_url)
  local url
  if parsed_url.query then
```

```
    url = parsed_url.path .. "?" .. parsed_url.query
  else
    url = parsed_url.path
  end

  local body =
    cjson_encode(
    {
      consumer = ngx.ctx.authenticated_consumer,
      api = ngx.ctx.api
    }
  )

  local headers =
    string_format(
    "%s %s HTTP/1.1\r\nHost: %s\r\nConnection: Keep-Alive\r
\nContent-Type: application/json\r\nContent-Length: %s\r\n",
    config.method:upper(),
    url,
    parsed_url.host,
    #body
  )

  return string_format("%s\r\n%s", headers, body)
end
```

`ngx.ctx` is a table that stores per-request Lua context data and has a life time identical to the current request. It's possible to add keys to the table (in order to share some requested data between plugins).

The message consists of two parts: headers and a body. Headers have a protocol, method, host, `content-type` set to `application/json` since we will send a JSON, `content-length`, and keep-alive set connection headers. The body is just a JSON encoded consumer (if it exists) and API tables.

Finally, we can send a message:

```
-- handler.lua
...
  ok, err = sock:send(get_message(config, parsed_url))
  if not ok then
    ngx.log(ngx.ERR, "[notification-log] failed to send data
to " .. host .. ":" .. tostring(port) .. ": ", err)
  end
```

When the message is sent, it's a good idea to set `keepalive`. It will put the current co-socket connection back to the pool so it can be used by another connection:

```
--handler.lua
...
  ok, err = sock:setkeepalive(config.keepalive)
  if not ok then
    ngx.log(ngx.ERR, "[notification-log] failed to keepalive
to " .. host .. ":" .. tostring(port) .. ": ", err)
    return
  end
```

It's worth mentioning that you can use functions from the other plugins and actually, from any Lua module from the Kong core and the libraries it depends upon. The list of Kong dependencies is available in the kong `rockspec` file.

The code logic is done. We parse a URL from the config, generate a message to send, create a TCP connection, and send that message to the remote server. We log errors on each possible point of failure. We use the `keepalive` configuration to return the connection back to the pool for better performance, and finally we use `timeout` to limit the waiting time for each of the socket operations.

Despite how it works, the code has a significant issue, it's synchronous. That means until we get a response from the remote server we notify, Kong won't send a response back to the client. The solution is to use `ngx.timer.at` with zero delay. It will run code asynchronously to the original context creating the timer.

```
-- handler.lua
function NotificationHandler:access(config)
  NotificationHandler.super.access(self)

  local ok, err = ngx.timer.at(0, send, config, ngx.ctx)
  if not ok then
    ngx.log(ngx.ERR, "failed to create timer: ", err)
    return
  end
end
```

Now, all of the core logic is in the send function:

```
-- handler.lua
function send(premature, config, ctx)
```

```
    -- do some routine job in Lua just like a cron job
    if premature then
      return
    end
    ...
  end
```

We moved `ngx.ctx` to a separate argument, since it won't be available directly in the asynchronous function. The rest of the logic doesn't change. Now we return upstream responses immediately to the client and do a notification request asynchronously.

Plugin migrations and Dao factory

Our plugin can send a notification request to the configured server with the API and consumer information. But we don't store anything in our system about that. We can add more logs, but it would not be easy to find them later without an external logging tool. For this plugin we will save events we're sending into the database, to be able to extend the Kong Admin API to search them.

Working with a database from a custom plugin starts with creating a migration for the database. We will support both databases, `postgres` and `cassandra`, but you can create a migration only for the database you will actually use (double square brackets in Lua used to enclose literal strings that traverse several lines):

```
kong-notification-plugin/kong/plugins/notification/migrations
├── postgres.lua
└── cassandra.lua

-- cassandra.lua
return {
  {
    name = "2018-01-27-841841_init_notification",
    up = [[
        CREATE TABLE IF NOT EXISTS notifications(
          id uuid,
          api_id uuid,
          consumer_id uuid,
          params text,
          timeout int,
          keepalive int,
          created_at timestamp,
          PRIMARY KEY (id)
```

```
        );
      ]],
    down = [[
        DROP TABLE notifications;
      ]]
  }
}

-- postgres.lua
return {
  {
    name = "2018-01-27-841841_init_notification",
    up = [[
        CREATE TABLE IF NOT EXISTS notifications(
          id uuid,
          api_id uuid REFERENCES apis (id),
          consumer_id uuid REFERENCES consumers (id),
          timeout integer,
          keepalive integer,
          params text,
          created_at timestamp without time zone default
(CURRENT_TIMESTAMP(0) at time zone 'utc'),
          PRIMARY KEY (id)
        );
      ]],
    down = [[
        DROP TABLE notifications;
      ]]
  }
}
```

Migrations are simply tables with `name`, `up`, and `down` keys:

- `name` is used to define which migrations Kong already applied (executed migrations saved into `schema_migrations` table).
- `up` - is the query for the forward change.
- `down` - is the query for the rollback change.

There is a different type of migration when it's required to update the plugin config in every place where it's applied. It's possible to write such migrations manually manipulating with JSON, but there is a better way: use the Kong migrations helper:

```
-- handler.lua
local plugin_config_iterator =
require("kong.dao.migrations.helpers").plugin_config_iterator
```

```
return {
  ...
  {
    name = "2018-01-28-841841_notification",
    up = function(_, _, dao)
      for ok, config, update in plugin_config_iterator(dao,
"notification") do
        if not ok then
          return config
        end
        config.keepalive = 60000
        local ok, err = update(config)
        if not ok then
          return err
        end
      end
    end,
    down = function(_, _, dao)
    end -- not implemented
  }
}
```

In the example above we set the **keepalive** config parameter to 60000 in each place where the plugin is applied.

Now, when the database is ready, it's required to create a so-called DAO object, which provides a layer of abstraction over the database table. In the code we will work with the DAO object, but on save or update it will be transformed to the appropriate database row and vice versa. Getting a row from the database will be transformed into a DAO object. It's possible to work with many tables from the same plugin, so the DAO module should return a table of DAO objects:

```
-- daos.lua
local SCHEMA = {
  primary_key = {"id"},
  table = "notifications",
  fields = {
    id = {type = "id", dao_insert_value = true},
    created_at = {type = "timestamp", immutable = true,
dao_insert_value = true},
    api_id = {type = "id", required = true, foreign =
"apis:id"},
    consumer_id = {type = "id", required = true, foreign =
"consumers:id"},
    params = {type = "string", required = true}
  }
}
```

```
return {notifications = SCHEMA} -- this plugin only results
in one custom DAO, named `notifications`
```

`dao_inserted_value`-means that the value will be inserted by the DAO itself. `immutable`-doesn't allow you to update the field. `foreign`-is a foreign key (postgres only).

In the same way we handled the plugin configuration, we defined fields with their types and additional options. Each field can have the same options as a field in `schema.lua` and some **new options are possible** (e.g.: `dao_insert_value`, `foreign`, and `primary_key`).

The notification plugin needs to save a message it sent to the remote server to the database. We load a DAO factory and get `notifications` for the DAO object as it's property. The DAO object has an `insert` function to create a new row in the database:

```
-- handler.lua
local singletons = require "kong.singletons"
local dao_factory = singletons.dao

local notifications_dao = dao_factory.notifications
local notification,
  err =
  notifications_dao:insert(
  {
    api_id = ngx.ctx.api_id,
    consumer_id =
ngx.ctx.authenticated_credential.consumer_id,
    params = message
  }
)
```

It's possible to work with core DAO objects (APIs, consumers, plugins), so we can query those tables from the plugin:

```
local singletons = require "kong.singletons"
local dao_factory = singletons.dao

local apis_dao = singletons.dao.apis
local consumers_dao = singletons.dao.consumers
local plugins_dao = singletons.dao.plugins
```

To do that just get a required DAO from the factory and use one of the existing query functions:

Function	Description
`DAO:count (tbl)`	Count the number of rows.
`DAO:delete (tbl)`	Delete a row.
`DAO:find (tbl)`	Find a row.
`DAO:find_all (tbl)`	Find all rows.
`DAO:find_page (tbl, page_offset, page_size)`	Find a paginated set of rows.
`DAO:insert (tbl, options)`	Insert a row.
`DAO:new (db, model_mt, schema, constraints)`	Instanciate a DAO.
`DAO:update (tbl, filter_keys, options)`	Update a row.

We have already learned how to create database migrations for the plugin tables and plugin configuration. Also, we used a DAO factory to save data into the plugin related table. One more extendable part of Kong we didn't touch yet is the Admin API.

Extending the Admin API

Once we write the requests to the Kong database, we should be able to read them. Of course it's possible querying the database directly, but Kong provides a convenient way to implement custom API endpoints, so we can create a basic CRUD set of operations around notifications.

Kong will load admin endpoints from the `api.lua` file, so let's create it. The plugin structure should now look like this:

```
kong-notification-plugin/kong/plugins/notification
├── migrations
├── api.lua
├── daos.lua
├── handler.lua
└── schema.lua
```

The API module should return a Lua table with a list of endpoint paths in keys and another table as values describing HTTP methods. You can think about it as executing this function (let's name it an `action`) for the given endpoint(s) on the given method. Each action receives these arguments:

- `self` - is the Lapis request object. We can get different useful information from it, like request params, cookies, headers, session, etc. The full list of supported parameters and methods is available in the **Lapis documentation**
- `dao_factory` - is the object we used to get the Dao for our plugin.
- `helpers` - a table with `responses` and `yield_error` keys. The full description is available at **Kong's documentation**.

For the notification plugin it might look like this:

```
-- api.lua
return {
  ["/notification"] = {
    GET = function(self, dao_factory, helpers)
      -- ...
    end
  }
}
```

Since we don't want to modify existing notifications in the database, we will implement the GET method. The desired response will be a paginated JSON list of notifications. For that we can use the Kong CRUD helpers module: `kong.api.crud_helpers`. It has a list of convenient functions to work with the Kong database and is completely compatible with the action's arguments:

```
-- api.lua
local crud = require "kong.api.crud_helpers"
```

Now, use the CRUD helpers function:

```
-- api.lua
...
    GET = function(self, dao_factory, helpers)
      crud.paginated_set(self, dao_factory.notifications)
    end
```

Wow, that looks very simple! And it is, since all of the work is done under the hood by Kong and the Lapis framework. It will process the request, get pagination params, create a database query to the notifications table, and return a JSON response to the client, all in a single line.

In response Kong will send a JSON with two fields:

```
{
    "data": [
        {
            "api_id": "adedc2c2-7e38-4327-ab15-448c511d705e",
            "created_at": 1517609518000,
            "id": "898b864c-c5fb-46dc-a003-837ac02fef86",
            "params": ...
        },
        ...
    ],
    "total": 15
}
```

`data` - actually holds a list of notifications `total` - total number of items by the given filter

By default Kong will return the first 100 rows from the database. To change the size of the page, just set the `size` query parameter:

```
curl -XGET "http://localhost:8001/notification?size=5"
```

That will return only five items:

```
{
    "data": [
        {
            "api_id": "adedc2c2-7e38-4327-ab15-448c511d705e",
            "created_at": 1517609518000,
            "id": "898b864c-c5fb-46dc-a003-837ac02fef86",
            "params": ...
        },
        ...
    ],
    "next": "http://localhost:8001/notification?offset=Mg%3D
%3D&size=5",
    "offset": "Mg==",
    "total": 15
}
```

The response has a different structure with a couple new fields:

`next` - is the link to the next page `offset` - Base64 encoded number of the next page

But what if we want to do some filter queries, like getting notifications by consumer or API? Kong has helpers for that too. Let's add another endpoint to get notifications by api_id:

```
-- api.lua
...
  ["/notification/api/:api_name_or_id"] = {
    GET = function(self, dao_factory, helpers)
      crud.paginated_set(self, dao_factory.notifications)
    end
  }
```

It looks the same, except the URL, and it won't work as expected, so we need to tell Kong somehow to apply `api_id` from the request to the database query. To accomplish it we will use the Lapis `before` callback. It applies to each request just before the action will be executed, so we can do some extra validations and modify `self.params`.

```
-- api.lua
...
  ["/notification/api/:api_name_or_id"] = {
    before = function(self, dao_factory, helpers)
      crud.find_api_by_name_or_id(self, dao_factory, helpers)
      self.params.api_id = self.api.id
    end,
```

Notice the `api_name_or_id` that is special and will be processed by the Kong CRUD helper. Once we set `api_id` to the params, the `paginated_set` helper will run a filter query to get notifications by `api_id` from the `params`.

In the same fashion we can implement a filter by `consumer_id`, except the `api_name_or_id`, which will change to `username_or_id`:

```
-- api.lua
...
  ["/notification/consumer/:username_or_id"] = {
    before = function(self, dao_factory, helpers)
      crud.find_consumer_by_username_or_id(self,
dao_factory, helpers)
      self.params.consumer_id = self.consumer.id
    end,

    GET = function(self, dao_factory, helpers)
      crud.paginated_set(self, dao_factory.notifications)
    end
  }
```

Similarly, it's easy to add a filter by both `api_id` and `consumer_id`, but the main change is in the routing:

```
-- api.lua
  ["/notification/api/:api_name_or_id/
consumer/:username_or_id"] = {
```

And before the callback (it will retrieve both the API and consumer from the database):

```
-- api.lua
    before = function(self, dao_factory, helpers)
      crud.find_api_by_name_or_id(self, dao_factory, helpers)
      crud.find_consumer_by_username_or_id(self,
dao_factory, helpers)
      self.params.api_id = self.api.id
      self.params.consumer_id = self.consumer.id
  end
```

In case the API or consumer was not found in the database, the Kong helper will return a 404 status code.

And don't forget we can still filter notifications by `api_id` or `consumer_id` at the `notification` URL just by sending the appropriate query params:

```
curl -XGET "http://localhost:8001/notification?
size=2&api_id=adedc2c2-7e38-4327-ab15-448c511d705e"
```

The Lapis framework allows you to render HTML, not only JSON. And again we have several options on how to do that.

We can render HTML directly in the action, such as:

```
-- api.lua
    GET = function(self, dao_factory, helpers)
      return self:html(
        function()
          h2("Notifications")
          element(
            "table",
            {},
            function()
              thead(
                function()
                  return tr(
                    function()
                      th("Id")
                      th("Api ID")
                      th("Consumer ID")
                      th("Created")
```

```
                    return th("Params")
                  end
                )
              end
            )
          end
        )
      end
    )
  end
```

Or we can use a **moonscript** and generate a Lua template from it. Detailed information is available at the moonscript website and **Lapis documentation**. Once the template is generated, we can use it in the action (Lapis layout is used as an example):

```
-- api.lua
  local template = require("lapis.views.layout")

  GET = function(self, dao_factory, helpers)
    return {render = template}
  end
```

Another way to render HTML is with **etlua**. It's a **template language** that compiles to Lua. To use it with Kong we need to enable it in the Lapis app and set a `views_prefix` to the directory where we will store templates:

```
-- api.lua
  GET = function(self, dao_factory, helpers)
    self.app:enable("etlua")
    self.app.views_prefix = "kong.plugins.notification.views"
    return {render = "index"}
  end
```

Then a simple template can look like this:

```
-- views/index.etlua
<div class="my_page">
  Here is a random number: <%= math.random() %>
</div>
```

We will use only JSON responses in the notification plugin, but it's good to know that any Kong plugin can be turned into a full HTML application.

Kong gives developers a lot for building a custom Admin API. Using the powerful Lapis framework with convenient helpers to work with database queries, you can build a paginated response, and even return HTML pages.

Execution order

Your plugin may depend on context, set by other plugins, especially if you depend on Kong core plugins. For that reason Kong has a plugin order priority, which defines plugin execution orders. It means that each plugin callback (`access`, `log`, `body_filter`, etc.) will be executed in each plugin by order, defined with order priority. For example, according to the **Kong documentation** an `access` callback will be executed in the `bot-detection` plugin first, then `cors`, etc.

To set the custom plugin priority, just set a `PRIORITY` value for the plugin handler:

```
-- handler.lua
NotificationHandler.PRIORITY = 0
```

The greater the priority, the earlier the plugin will be executed. For our notification plugin it's fine to set the lowest priority.

It's also possible to modify the priority of other plugins, but it should be done extremely carefully and in rare cases, since it will affect the whole execution order and may break things. For example, the code below will change the priority of the `correlation-id` plugin:

```
-- handler.lua
CorrelationIdHandler.PRIORITY = 1501
```

Plugin testing

Lua is a great programming language, but like any programming language it's not perfect. Since its a scripting language, all of the exceptions are happening durin runtime. Furthermore, it's absolutely required to understand if the plugin we wrote does the task it's supposed to do. The first step to make sure that a plugin actually works is to load it to Kong. In the case of syntax errors it will be noticed and Kong won't start. The next step is to add the plugin to the API and try to hit it under different conditions. If everything works fine, then we're lucky and wrote the perfect code on the first try. Otherwise, we will get a 500 status code response from Kong and exception stacktrace in the logs. Usually the code we write is not perfect and testing different conditions manually takes time and is not convenient. It may take a while to make sure that the plugin works correctly for all cases, but there is a better solution: writing tests.

We may write two basic types of Kong plugin tests: unit and integration.

UNIT TESTS

Unit tests are usually used for business logic, which has no Kong context, and **pure functions** is a perfect example. Each test is just a call of a function we want to test under some condition. We check that it returns an expected result, otherwise the test will fail. Lua has many different testing frameworks, but Kong documentation suggests to use **busted**, which we will use for both: unit and integration tests. It's easier to run tests locally, but we will consider resting in our Docker environment as well.

First, we need to install `busted` locally:

```
luarocks install busted
```

Second, copy `bin/busted` from the Kong repository to the plugin directory. It will allow you to test the plugin code with all of its dependencies. To test the `parse_url` function we need to make it callable from outside the `handler.lua`:

```
-- handler.lua
function NotificationHandler:parse_url(raw_url)
...
end
```

That way we can call it in the test module directly. By default, `busted` will run test files with the `_spec` suffix, so we can create a `handler_spec.lua` inside the `specs` directory:

```
kong-notification-plugin
└── bin
  └── busted
└── kong
  └── plugins
    └── notification
      ├── migrations
      ├── api.lua
```

```
        ├── daos.lua
        ├── handler.lua
        └── schema.lua
  └── specs
    └── handler_spec.lua
```

Let's write a few tests for parsing regular URL, HTTPS, and invalid URL. Testing with `busted` is simple: the `describe` function defines a context and takes name and function arguments; `it` function defines a test that receives a test name and a function to execute. Context allows you to group tests, add tags, insulate or expose environment, etc:

```
-- handler_spec.lua
local handler = require("kong.plugins.notification.handler")

describe(
  "testing parse_url #unit",
  function()
    it(
      "test success http",
      function()
        local parsed_url = handler:parse_url("http://
localhost/test?query=param")
        assert.are.same(
          {
            host = "localhost",
            port = 80,
            path = "/test",
            query = "query=param",
            scheme = "http",
            authority = "localhost"
          },
          parsed_url
        )
      end
    )

    it(
      "test success https",
      function()
        local parsed_url = handler:parse_url("https://
localhost/test")
        assert.are.same(
          {
            host = "localhost",
            port = 443,
            path = "/test",
```

```
            scheme = "https",
            authority = "localhost"
          },
          parsed_url
        )
      end
    )

    it(
      "test parse invalid url",
      function()
        local parsed_url = handler:parse_url("invalid")
        assert.are.same(
          {
            path = "invalid"
          },
          parsed_url
        )
      end
    )
  end
)
```

In each of the tests above we call the `parse_url` method handler with a URL and assert that the result is equal as expected. The full list of assertions is available at **busted documentation**. We used a tag `unit` defined in the describe title as `#unit` for later usage.

To run the tests just call the `bin/busted` with the path to the test file as an argument:

```
$ bin/busted spec/handler_spec.lua
***
3 successes / 0 failures / 0 errors / 0 pending : 0.002079
seconds
```

Tests are passed, so now it's time to test the `get_message` function, but first we have to make it callable from the outside:

```
-- handler.lua
function NotificationHandler:get_message(config, parsed_url)
...
end
```

Let's add a success `get_message` test:

```
-- handler_spec.lua
describe(
  "testing get_message #unit",
  function()
    it(
      "test success get_message no query",
      function()
        local config = {method = "GET"}
        local parsed_url = {host = "localhost", path = "/
test"}
        ngx.ctx = {authenticated_consumer = {id = 1}, api =
{id = 1}}
        local message = handler:get_message(config,
parsed_url)
        local body = [[{"consumer":{"id":1},"api":{"id":1}}]]
        local expected_message =
          string_format(
          "%s %s HTTP/1.1\r\nHost: %s\r\nConnection: Keep-
Alive\r\nContent-Type: application/json\r\nContent-Length: %s
\r\n\r\n%s",
          "GET",
          "/test",
          "localhost",
          #body,
          body
        )
        assert.are.same(expected_message, message)
      end
    )
  end
)
```

Notice the usage of `ngx.ctx`. We can set values that will be used in the handler. We can also test that it fails to get a message if `ngx.ctx` is nil or config is nil, etc:

```
-- handler_spec.lua
describe(
  "testing get_message #unit",
  ...
    it(
      "test fail get_message ctx is nil",
      function()
        ngx.ctx = nil
        assert.has.errors(
          function()
            handler:get_message({}, {})
          end
```

```
        )
      end
    )

    it(
      "test fail get_message ctx is nil",
      function()
        local config = nil
        ngx.ctx = {authenticated_consumer = {id = 1}, api =
{id = 1}}
        assert.has.errors(
          function()
            handler:get_message(nil, {})
          end
        )
      end
    )
end
```

To run tests with specified tags use the `--tags` option:

```
$ bin/busted --tags=unit
******
6 successes / 0 failures / 0 errors / 0 pending : 0.043482
seconds
```

To run tests in Docker we need to do some preparations:

```
RUN luarocks install busted
RUN ln -s /usr/local/openresty/bin/resty /usr/local/bin/resty
RUN mkdir -p /home/kong/bin
RUN mkdir -p /home/kong/spec

COPY busted /home/kong/bin/busted
RUN chmod 755 /home/kong/bin/busted
```

We also installed `busted` from `luarocks`, adding `resty` to $PATH, creating directories to store a `busted` script from Kong and our tests, then we copy `busted` into the image, and finally we set permissions.

Also, we can add volume with tests from our plugin directory:

```
services:
  ...
  kong:
    build: ./kong
    volumes:
      - ../kong-notification-plugin/kong/plugins/
```

```
notification:/usr/local/share/lua/5.1/kong/plugins/
notification:ro
      - ../kong-notification-plugin/spec/handler_spec.lua:/
home/kong/spec/handler_spec.lua:ro
    ...
```

To run the tests we need to start the container, `exec` into it and run `bin/busted` from the `/home/kong` directory. `/home/kong` is not special. You can choose any directory, you only need to be sure it will have the `bin/busted` script and the `spec` directory with tests:

```
 docker ps | grep "kongbookexample_kong" | head -1 | cut -d'
' -f1
 docker exec -it 70f93e33186f sh
/ # cd home/kong/
/home/kong # bin/busted --tags=unit
******
6 successes / 0 failures / 0 errors / 0 pending : 0.005295
seconds
```

INTEGRATION TESTS

The next step is to create integration tests that will actually start the Kong and hit its endpoints. To achieve that locally, we need to copy `spec/helpers.lua` and `spec/kong_tests.conf` files from the Kong source into the plugin root directory. In `helpers.lua` we may change the BIN_PATH variable to the path of your Kong executable (depends on your Kong installation). For example, you can have `kong` locally in the path, and `bin/kong` won't work, so set it to just `kong`:

```
-- helpers.lua
local BIN_PATH = "kong"
...
```

You also may change `kong_tests.conf` to match your desired testing configuration, e.g. set the database, hosts, and ports. Just disable SSL support and custom DNS hostfiles for simplicity by commenting appropriate lines out and adding notification plugins to custom_plugins:

```
-- kong_tests.conf
# ssl_cert = spec/fixtures/kong_spec.crt
# ssl_cert_key = spec/fixtures/kong_spec.key

# admin_ssl_cert = spec/fixtures/kong_spec.crt
```

```
# admin_ssl_cert_key = spec/fixtures/kong_spec.key
...
# dns_hostsfile = spec/fixtures/hosts
custom_plugins = notification
```

The next step is to create test database migrations. We run the Kong migrations command with our test configuration and `notification` plugin enabled:

```
KONG_CUSTOM_PLUGINS=notification kong migrations up -c spec/
kong_tests.conf
```

Finally, we can write an integration test. The first algorithm is just to test that we can apply a plugin to the API and hit that API without errors. As a test template, we will use one from the **Kong official documentation** and modify it a bit:

```
-- 01-access_spec.lua
local helpers = require "spec.helpers"

describe(
  "notification plugin #integration",
  function()
    local proxy_client
    local admin_client
    setup(
      function()
        assert(
          helpers.dao.apis:insert {
            name = "test-api",
            method = "GET",
            upstream_url = "https://www.google.com"
          }
        )
        -- start Kong with your testing Kong configuration
(defined in "spec.helpers")
        assert(helpers.start_kong({custom_plugins =
"notification"}))
        admin_client = helpers.admin_client()
      end
    )
    teardown(
      function()
        if admin_client then
          admin_client:close()
        end
        helpers.stop_kong()
```

```
      end
    )
    before_each(
      function()
        proxy_client = helpers.proxy_client()
      end
    )
    after_each(
      function()
        if proxy_client then
          proxy_client:close()
        end
      end
    )
```

In this test we insert a single API into the database and start Kong with the `notification` plugin enabled. We also start the Admin API.

In the test we need to make sure we can add our plugin to the endpoint, hit that endpoint, and check that the request was written to the `notifications` table by accessing the Admin API:

```
-- 01-access_spec.lua
...
    describe(
      "add notification plugin",
      function()
        it(
          "success add notification plugin to api",
          function()
            -- add notification plugin to api
            local res =
              assert(
                add
              admin_client:send {
                method = "POST",
                path = "/apis/" .. api.id .. "/plugins/",
                body = {
                  name = "notification",
                  config = {
                    url = "http://127.0.0.1:9001/",
                    method = "GET"
                  }
                },
                headers = {
                  ["Content-Type"] = "application/json"
                }
              }
```

```
            )
            assert.res_status(201, res)

            -- hit api
            local res =
              assert(
              proxy_client:send {
                method = "GET",
                path = "/test"
              }
            )
            assert.res_status(200, res)
            -- get notifications from the database
            local res =
              admin_client:send {
              method = "GET",
              path = "/notification",
              headers = {
                ["Content-Type"] = "application/json"
              }
            }

            local body = cjson.decode(assert.res_status(200,
res))
            assert.equal(1, body.total)
          end
        )
      end
    )
```

The test looks complex, but basically it just has three requests and assertions, and the latest response has a single notification in it. It's worth noticing, that Kong clean tests databases after each testing, so when tests are passed we won't see any APIs or notifications in the database. The invalid config is simpler:

```
-- 01-access_spec.lua
...
        it(
          "fail to add notification plugin without url",
          function()
            local res =
              assert(
              admin_client:send {
                method = "POST",
                path = "/apis/" .. api.id .. "/plugins/",
                body = {
                  name = "notification",
```

```
                config = {
                  method = "GET"
                }
              },
              headers = {
                ["Content-Type"] = "application/json"
              }
            }
          )
          local body = assert.res_status(400, res)
          local json = cjson.decode(body)
          assert.same({["config.url"] = "url is
required"}, json)
        end
      )

      it(
        "fail to add notification plugin without method",
        function()
          local res =
            assert(
            admin_client:send {
              method = "POST",
              path = "/apis/" .. api.id .. "/plugins/",
              body = {
                name = "notification",
                config = {
                  url = "http://127.0.0.1:9001/"
                }
              },
              headers = {
                ["Content-Type"] = "application/json"
              }
            }
          )
          local body = assert.res_status(400, res)
          local json = cjson.decode(body)
          assert.same({["config.method"] = "method is
required"}, json)
        end
      )
    end
...
```

We send a single request and assert appropriate error messages in the response. Now it’s time to run the tests:

```
$ bin/busted --tags=integration
***
3 successes / 0 failures / 0 errors / 0 pending : 4.76591
seconds
```

Integration testing in Docker is more complicated, but still possible. First, we need to setup a tests database to not pollute our kong database:

```
services:
  ...
  kong-postgres-test:
    image: postgres:alpine
    environment:
      - POSTGRES_DB=kong_tests
      - POSTGRES_USER=kong
    ports:
      - "5434:5432"
```

It's a copy of our database service, but exposes a different port: 5434. Next we need to setup a separate migration service:

```
services:
  ...
  kong-migration-test:
    build: ./kong
    volumes:
      - ../kong-notification-plugin/kong/plugins/
notification:/usr/local/share/lua/5.1/kong/plugins/
notification:ro
    links:
      - kong-postgres-test
    environment:
      - KONG_DATABASE=postgres
      - KONG_PG_HOST=kong-postgres-test
      - KONG_PG_DATABASE=kong_tests
      - KONG_CUSTOM_PLUGINS=notification
    command: kong migrations up
```

It's similar to our migration service, but uses our new kong_tests database. Next, we need to update a kong service adding a volume with integration tests, links to the test database, and a dependency from the kong-migration-test service:

```
services:
  ...
```

```
  kong:
    volumes:
      ...
      - ../kong-notification-plugin/spec/01-access_spec.lua:/
home/kong/spec/01-access_spec.lua:ro
    links:
      ...
      - kong-postgres-test
    depends_on:
      - kong-migration
      - kong-migration-test
```

Finally, we need to add `helpers.lua` and `kong_tests.conf` to the `/home/kong/spec` directory in our image:

```
COPY helpers.lua /home/kong/spec/helpers.lua
COPY kong_tests.conf /home/kong/spec/kong_tests.conf
```

The `helpers.lua` is the same as we used for local testing, but `kong_tests.conf` has different `admin_listen_ssl` and `dns_resolver` values:

```
# kong_tests.conf
admin_listen_ssl = 127.0.0.1:8445
dns_resolver = 127.0.0.11
```

Notice the `dns_resolver` value. Just run the simple command inside the running container:

```
/ # grep nameserver /etc/resolv.conf | cut -d ' ' -f 2
127.0.0.11
```

Once all the preparations are done, we can run the tests:

```
/home/kong # bin/busted
*********
9 successes / 0 failures / 0 errors / 0 pending : 0.958038
seconds
```

Everything works! That's it for testing. We wrote unit and integration tests, tested success and failure cases, both locally and in the Docker environment. Now it will be much easier to change plugins in the future without worrying about breaking anything. Despite integration tests requiring some preparation work, it's worth it. Manual testing is much slower and not so reliable. Also, the way to setup integration tests may change in the future. For instance, a suite of testing tools, independent of the main Kong repository, may be released, but until that happens a custom solution is required.

Share it with luarocks

Once the plugin is done and tested, it is time to share it with the world. For that task we will use `luarocks`. The process consists of three steps:

1. Creating a `rockspec` file
2. Creating an `api-key` at `https://luarocks.org`
3. Running `luarocks upload` to create a `rock` file based on `rockspec`, and upload it to the luarocks repository

A `rockspec` file has the description of the package, source, and dependencies, along with information with files to compile:

```
-- kong-plugin-notification-0.1.0-1.rockspec
package = "kong-plugin-notification"

version = "0.1.0-1"

supported_platforms = {"linux", "macosx"}

source = {
  url = "git://github.com/backstopmedia/kong-book-example",
  tag = "0.1.0",
  branch = "notification"
}

description = {
  summary = "A simple notification plugin",
  homepage = "http://getkong.org",
  license = "MIT"
}

dependencies = {}

local pluginName = "notification"
local prefix = "kong.plugins."..pluginName
build = {
  type = "builtin",
  modules = {
    [prefix..".migrations.cassandra"] = "kong/
plugins/"..pluginName.."/migrations/cassandra.lua",
    [predix..".migrations.postgres"] = "kong/
```

```
plugins/"..pluginName.."/migrations/postgres.lua",
    [prefix..".handler"] = "kong/plugins/"..pluginName.."/
handler.lua",
    [prefix..".schema"] = "kong/plugins/"..pluginName.."/
schema.lua",
    [prefix..".api"] = "kong/plugins/"..pluginName.."/
api.lua",
    [prefix..".daos"] = "kong/plugins/"..pluginName.."/
daos.lua",
  }
}
```

There are some naming requirements:

- The package name should match the prefix of the `rockspec` filename, but the `kong-plugin` prefix is used as a convention.
- The version should match the version in the `rockspec` filename too. The trailing `1` is the version of the `rockspec` file itself.

We should enumerate all modules that are the part of the plugin in the `build` section, since the modules not included in that table won't be available after publishing the plugin. Notice the `source` field that is required and we will use a Github repository as a source. The full description of the `rockspec` format is available in the **luarocks documentation**.

Once `rockspec` is ready, we need to have an `api-key` to upload it to the luarocks repository. To do that sign up at **https://luarocks.org** and generate a key at `https://luarocks.org/settings/api-keys`. The last step is to upload the plugin:

```
luarocks upload kong-plugin-notification-0.1.0-1.rockspec --
api-key=<your api key>
```

If you uploaded the wrong code, it's possible to overwrite an existing version at the luarocks repository, so just use a `--force` key:

```
luarocks upload kong-plugin-notification-0.1.0-1.rockspec --
api-key=<your api key> --force
```

Summary

In this chapter we discussed how to install and enable Kong plugins in the system, we built a custom notification plugin from scratch, and shared it with the community via luarocks. The final source code is available at **github**. The plugin sends an asynchronous request to the remote server, saves data in its own database table, and modifies the Kong Admin API by adding new endpoints to search notifications in a convenient way. Kong supports building HTML pages in the Admin API, and we discussed several options of how to do that. Unit and integration tests helped to make sure everything works as expected and we covered basic plugin use cases with them.

So, Kong provides a very powerful, flexible and convenient interface for writing custom plugins of any complexity, and even without Lua knowledge it's possible to write one in a sane period of time.

Integrating with others 7

Until now, we've looked over Kong's powerful functionality. It's obvious that Kong excels with managing the APIs, but it can't cover up all of the DevOps by itself. Because of this, in this chapter, we'll introduce some of the integrations for Kong to cover up DevOps efficiently.

Additionally, we'll cover some of the integrations that help you with configuring Kong without typing commands on terminal.

All of the code for the sample project in this book can be found **here**.

Deployment

So far we've used Kong by simply installing on the host, but installing it isn't the best way in some cases.

For example, let's say that you're running lots of instances on a server and you need to install and configure Kong on your entire host. Those tasks are repeated over and over again and consume a lot of time.
Or let's say you have to scale your server and it has to be done in the identically same environment. It's pretty hard to configure the same environment because it has a dependency with the host operating system.

In situations like this, there are some better ways to deploy, and some candidates for this situation are `Docker` and `Kubernetes`. In this section, we'll look over how to deploy our services and Kong with other options, and how to configure them.

Docker

Docker is a Linux container based on an open source virtualization platform. A container is an isolated process that is an encapsulated form of an application and its dependencies. Based on this, Docker brings lots of benefits to DevOps.

- Container shares resources from the host os
  - Compared to the virtual machine, resources are used much more efficient.
- Isolated from the host os
  - It doesn't affect the host, which means it has great portability
- Container's Linux kernel sharing architecture
  - Due to Lightweight architecture, it can be run blazingly fast.
- Easy to build, ship, and run distributed applications
  - Dependency and configurations are contained in one. So any other installs or configures aren't needed.

INSTALLATION

Issue the following command to install Docker.

```
curl -fsSL https://download.docker.com/linux/ubuntu/gpg |
sudo apt-key add -
sudo add-apt-repository "deb [arch=amd64] https://
download.docker.com/linux/ubuntu $(lsb_release -cs) stable"
sudo apt-get update
sudo apt-get install -y docker-ce
```

The Docker command needs root privileges by default. But If you don't want to type `sudo` with each command, adding the user in the Docker group allows you to issue the `docker` command without `sudo`.

```
sudo usermod -aG docker ${USER}
su - ${USER}
```

To verify that `docker` is installed properly, run a simple Docker image, `hello-world`.

```
docker run hello-world

Unable to find image 'hello-world:latest' locally
latest: Pulling from library/hello-world
ca4f61b1923c: Pull complete
Digest: sha256:ca0eeb6fb05351dfc8759c20733c91def84cb8007aa89
a5bf606bc8b315b9fc7
Status: Downloaded newer image for hello-world:latest

Hello from Docker!
This message shows that your installation appears to be
```

```
working correctly.
...
```

DEPLOY SERVICES

To deploy a container with Docker, first, we have to build a container image with `Dockerfile`. `Dockerfile` is a file that describes how to build a container image such as details about setting up an application. Below is an example of `Dockerfile`.

```
FROM python:alpine

WORKDIR /usr/src/app

COPY . .w
RUN pip install --no-cache-dir -r requirements.txt

ENTRYPOINT ["python"]

CMD ["app.py"]
```

We've created a `Dockerfile` for you in each of `cinema's` microservices folder. Move your directory into the `movies` microservice folder, and you can start building up containers.

```
# from your cinema working directory, change directory to
each microservices
cd movies
docker build -t "cinema:movies" .

Sending build context to Docker daemon  7.168kB
Step 1/6 : FROM python:alpine
 ---> 29b5ce58cfbc
Step 2/6 : WORKDIR /usr/src/app
 ---> 5640e81529c0
Step 3/6 : COPY . .
 ---> 5c62e72f7d3d
Step 4/6 : RUN pip install --no-cache-dir -r requirements.txt
 ---> Running in 5a7d78e988af
Collecting flask==0.12 (from -r requirements.txt (line 1))
...... output truncated ......
Removing intermediate container 5a7d78e988af
 ---> 83cc65606f99
Step 5/6 : ENTRYPOINT ["python"]
 ---> Running in 48ad756f3ff8
Removing intermediate container 48ad756f3ff8
```

```
 ---> 0732b6c1df93
Step 6/6 : CMD ["app.py"]
 ---> Running in f6babb5dbbbe
Removing intermediate container f6babb5dbbbe
 ---> c78beadd2f69
Successfully built c78beadd2f69
Successfully tagged cinema:movies
```

You've just created Docker images tagged with `cinema:movies`. To start the Docker image:

```
docker run -d --name cinema_movies \
    -p <movies_port>:5000 \
    cinema:movies
```

By issuing the command below, verify that the `cinema` movies microservice has been running properly.

```
curl localhost:<movies_port>

{
    "subresource_uris": {
        "movie": "/movies/<id>",
        "movies": "/movies"
    },
    "uri": "/"
}
```

Let's run all the other microservices. Be aware that the `users` container runs a bit different with others since `Users` microservice needs `movies` and the `bookings` service.

```
 # from your cinema working directory
cd bookings
docker build -t "cinema:bookings" .
docker run -d --name cinema_bookings \
    -p <bookings_port>:5000 \
    cinema:bookings
 # from your cinema working directory
cd showtimes
docker build -t "cinema:showtimes" .
docker run -d --name cinema_showtimes \
    -p <showtimes_port>:5000 \
    cinema:showtimes
 # from your cinema working directory
cd users
```

```
docker build -t "cinema:users" .
docker run -d --name cinema_users \
    --link cinema_bookings:bookings \
    --link cinema_movies:movies \
    -p <users_port>:5000 \
    cinema:users
```

By default, since containers reside independently from the host, each of the containers can't communicate with others. To make containers communicate, you have to use the `--link <name or id>:alias` option for the target container when you run it. The `--link cinema_bookings:bookings` option describes the link `cinema_bookings` container with the current container, and `cinema_bookings` will be called as the `bookings` alias.

More details about docker commands can be found **here**.

DEPLOY KONG

Before you run Kong, prepare your database with Docker or create your own. Here, we'll provision a database with Docker.

```
docker run -d --name kong-database \
                -p 5432:5432 \
                -e "POSTGRES_USER=kong" \
                -e "POSTGRES_DB=kong" \
                postgres:9.5

docker run --rm \
    --link kong-database:kong-database \
    -e "KONG_DATABASE=postgres" \
    -e "KONG_PG_HOST=kong-database" \
    kong kong migrations up

migrating core for database kong
core migrated up to: 2015-01-12-175310_skeleton
...... output truncated ......
oauth2 migrated up to: 2017-10-11-
oauth2_new_refresh_token_ttl_config_value
58 migrations ran
```

After provisioning your database, run Kong Docker with each microservice linked with it.

```
docker run -d --name kong \
  --link kong-database:kong-database \
```

```
    --link cinema_showtimes:showtimes \
    --link cinema_bookings:bookings \
    --link cinema_movies:movies \
    --link cinema_users:users \
    -e "KONG_DATABASE=postgres" \
    -e "KONG_PG_HOST=kong-database" \
    -e "KONG_PROXY_ACCESS_LOG=/dev/stdout" \
    -e "KONG_ADMIN_ACCESS_LOG=/dev/stdout" \
    -e "KONG_PROXY_ERROR_LOG=/dev/stderr" \
    -e "KONG_ADMIN_ERROR_LOG=/dev/stderr" \
    -e "KONG_ADMIN_LISTEN=0.0.0.0:8001" \
    -e "KONG_ADMIN_LISTEN_SSL=0.0.0.0:8444" \
    -p 8000:8000 \
    -p 8443:8443 \
    -p 8001:8001 \
    -p 8444:8444 \
    kong
```

To check that Kong has deployed successfully issue the command below.

```
> curl $(minikube service kong --url)
{"message": "no API found with those values"
```

CREATING API

From here you can start Kong with `8000` and `8001`. As we linked each microservices with aliases, each microservice can be called through `<alias>:5000`. To verify it, run curl commands with `docker exec` to pass the command to the container.

```
docker exec -it kong curl movies:5000

{
    "subresource_uris": {
        "movie": "/movies/<id>",
        "movies": "/movies"
    },
    "uri": "/"
}
```

Each of the services are accessible through `<alias>:5000`. For this reason, when adding API to Kong in Docker, we must specify each upstream URL with `<alias>:5000`.

```
curl -i -X POST http://localhost:8001/apis/ \
 --data 'name=movies' \
 --data 'hosts=cinema.com' \
 --data 'uris=/movies' \
 --data 'upstream_url=http://movies:5000'
```

Let's check whether it works correctly with the upstream_url.

```
curl -X GET http://localhost:8000/movies \
  --header 'Host: cinema.com'

{
    "subresource_uris": {
        "movie": "/movies/<id>",
        "movies": "/movies"
    },
    "uri": "/"
}
```

Congratulations! We've just created the first API with Kong in the Docker environment!

Kubernetes

Kubernetes is a container orchestration tool for automating deployment, scaling, and management of containerized applications. By grouping containers into logical units, managing containers becomes much easier. Kubernetes is built upon Google's 15 years of experience of running production.

Kubernetes can help you in several ways:

- Container orchestration
  - Resolves container deployment within the multiple hosts by decoupling resources, networking, etc. from the users.
- Manage containerized applications
  - Auto places containers in a suitable host; auto restarts the container in an unstable situation.
- Scaling, Replication, Rolling update, Rollback, etc.

To get started, first you need to create a Kubernetes cluster. Options are using cloud provider's Kubernetes service, creating your own cluster, or launching the pre-configured cluster with minikube.

In this section, we'll be using minikube for the Kubernetes cluster and launch our microservices and Kong.

INSTALLATION

For run commands against Kubernetes, a command line tool, kubectl, is required. Issue the below command to install `kubectl`.

```
curl -LO https://storage.googleapis.com/kubernetes-release/
release/v1.9.3/bin/linux/amd64/kubectl
chmod +x kubectl
sudo mv kubectl /usr/local/bin/kubectl
```

To verify that `kubectl` is installed correctly, issue `kubectl` on command. It'll describe the available commands with it.

```
kubectl controls the Kubernetes cluster manager.
Find more information at https://github.com/kubernetes/
kubernetes.
Basic Commands (Beginner):
  create         Create a resource from a file or from stdin.
  expose         Take a replication controller, service,
deployment or pod and expose it as a new Kubernetes Service
  run            Run a particular image on the cluster
  set            Set specific features on objects
...... output truncated ......

Use "kubectl <command> --help" for more information about a
given command.
Use "kubectl options" for a list of global command-line
options (applies to all commands).
```

Since we don't have a Kubernetes cluster yet, prior to sending commands with kubectl, install minikube first.

Before installing minikube, you need a Hypervisor in your host. Available options are VirtualBox, VMware, etc.

```
curl -Lo minikube https://storage.googleapis.com/minikube/
releases/v0.25.0/minikube-linux-amd64
chmod +x minikube
sudo mv minikube /usr/local/bin/
```

To start the Kubernetes cluster, issue `minikube start`.

```
Starting local Kubernetes v1.9.0 cluster...
Starting VM...
Downloading Minikube ISO
 142.22 MB / 142.22 MB
[============================================] 100.00% 0s
```

```
Getting VM IP
address...
Moving files into
cluster...
Downloading localkube
binary
 162.41 MB / 162.41 MB
[==========================================] 100.00%
0s
Setting up
certs...
Connecting to
cluster...
Setting up
kubeconfig...
Starting cluster components...
Kubectl is now configured to use the cluster.
Loading cached images from config file.
```

The command will download a new Virtual Host with hypervisor and creates Kubernetes Host. To use the minikube Kubernetes cluster and verify it, issue the command below.

```
> kubectl config use-context minikube
Switched to context "minikube".
> kubectl cluster-info
Kubernetes master is running at https://192.168.99.101:8443

To further debug and diagnose cluster problems, use 'kubectl
cluster-info dump'.
```

DEPLOY YOUR SERVICES

Before we deploy, let's briefly look over how Kubernetes works.

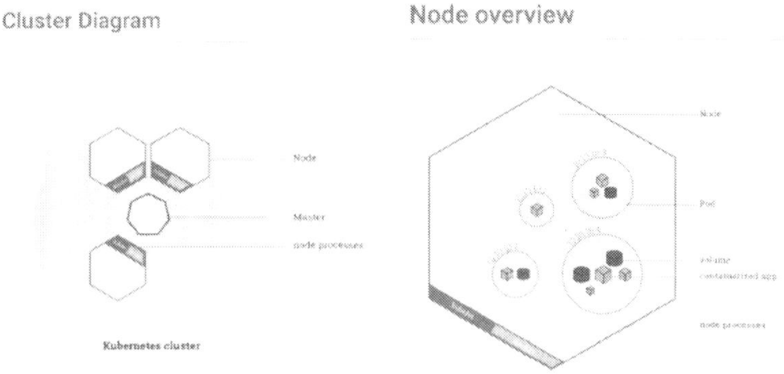

A Kubernetes cluster is constructed with multiple nodes, which is another host, and nodes are constructed with lots of `pods`, which is a logical group of container applications. `pods` are deployed through `Deployment`, and these deployed containers are accessible through `service`, which helps the container to be exposed publicly.

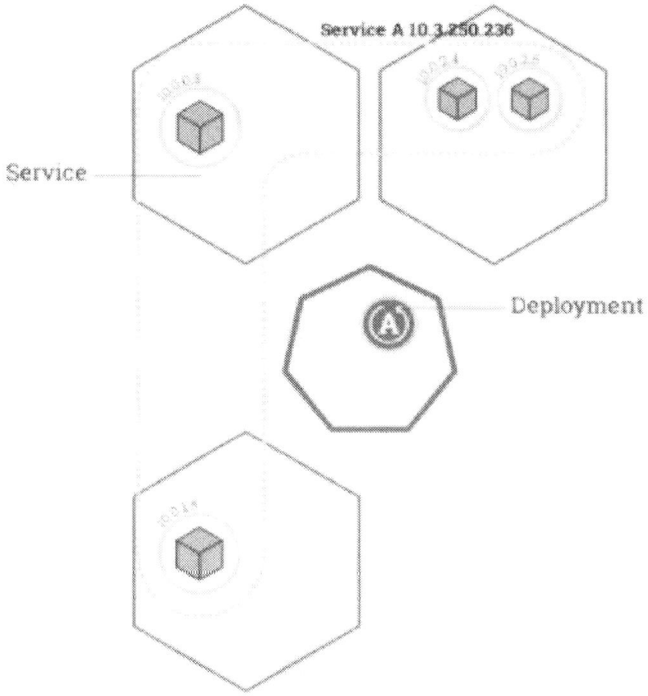

Here, we'll deploy our cinema microservice with Kubernetes, and access it through service. Since minikube can't fetch the images of the host docker, we'll re-build the image for the minikube and deploy to minikube.

```
# from your cinema working directory, change directory to
each microservices
cd movies
eval $(minikube docker-env)
docker build -t cinema:movies .
```

We've just built an image for minikube. Now to deploy our service, create a file `movies.yaml`, and fill the content like this.

```
# movies.yaml
apiVersion: v1
kind: Service
metadata:
```

```
  name: movies
spec:
  type: LoadBalancer
  ports:
  - port: 5000
  selector:
    app: movies
---
apiVersion: extensions/v1beta1
kind: Deployment
metadata:
  name: cinema-movies
spec:
  replicas: 1
  template:
    metadata:
      labels:
        name: movies
        app: movies
    spec:
      containers:
      - name: cinema-movies
        image: cinema:movies
        imagePullPolicy: Never
        ports:
        - containerPort: 5000
---
```

It creates a `deployment` of cinema-movies, and exposes this container with `movies` service. To launch a deployment, issue `kubectl create`.

```
kubectl create -f movies.yaml

service "movies" created
deployment "cinema-movies" deleted
```

To verify that our service has been deployed correctly, issue `kubectl get all` to check all of the deployment and services.

```
kubectl get all


NAME                       DESIRED   CURRENT   UP-TO-DATE
AVAILABLE   AGE
deploy/cinema-movies       1         1         1
1           6s
```

```
...... output truncated ......

NAME                                READY     STATUS
RESTARTS   AGE
po/cinema-movies-dc8fd748-2bqbk     1/1       Running
0          6s
...... output truncated ......

NAME                 TYPE           CLUSTER-IP
EXTERNAL-IP   PORT(S)          AGE
svc/movies           LoadBalancer   10.99.224.193
<pending>     5000:32498/TCP   16m
...... output truncated ......
```

To access our `movies` microservice container, issue a command with `minikube service <svc_name> --url`.

```
curl $(minikube service movies --url)

{
    "subresource_uris": {
        "movie": "/movies/<id>",
        "movies": "/movies"
    },
    "uri": "/"
}
```

DEPLOY KONG

Follow the instructions to start the Kong Kubernetes deployment **here**.

```
git clone git@github.com:Kong/kong-dist-kubernetes.git
cd kong-dist-kubernetes

kubectl create -f postgres.yaml
kubectl create -f kong_migration_postgres.yaml
kubectl create -f kong_postgres.yaml
```

It will create postgres Kubernetes deployment, prepare the datastore with `kong_migration_postgres`, and finally deploy the Kong. To check whether Kong is deployed correctly, issue `kubectl get all`.

```
kubectl get all

NAME               DESIRED   CURRENT   UP-TO-DATE
AVAILABLE   AGE
```

```
deploy/kong-rc   3          3          3
3           25s

...... output truncated ......

NAME                           READY     STATUS    RESTARTS
AGE
po/kong-rc-6bc75bc959-n224l   1/1       Running   0
25s
po/kong-rc-6bc75bc959-pkr9q   1/1       Running   0
25s
po/kong-rc-6bc75bc959-vwgs4   1/1       Running   0
25s
po/postgres-z9nnp             1/1       Running   0
46m

NAME                    TYPE            CLUSTER-IP
EXTERNAL-IP   PORT(S)          AGE
svc/kong-admin         LoadBalancer   10.97.39.131
<pending>     8001:32292/TCP   25s
svc/kong-admin-ssl     LoadBalancer   10.109.226.134
<pending>     8444:30999/TCP   25s
svc/kong-proxy         LoadBalancer   10.100.167.232
<pending>     8000:31927/TCP   25s
svc/kong-proxy-ssl     LoadBalancer   10.106.129.233
<pending>     8443:31133/TCP   25s
...... output truncated ......
```

You can check three instances if Kong is running on each pod. By issuing the below command, you can access Kong and kong-admin.

```
> curl $(minikube service kong-proxy --url)
{"message": "no API found with those values"}
> curl $(minikube service kong-admin --url)
{
  "version": "0.12.1",
  "plugins": {
...... output truncated ......
  },
  "tagline": "Welcome to kong",
  "configuration": {
...... output truncated ......
  },
  "lua_version": "LuaJIT 2.1.0-beta3",
  "hostname": "Kong"
}
```

CREATING AN API

From now you can start Kong with `$(minikube service <svc_name> --url)`. Similar to Docker, each microservices can be accessible through `<svc_name>:5000`. For this reason, when adding API to Kong in Kubernetes, we must specify each upstream url with `<svc_name>:5000`.

```
curl -i -X POST $(minikube service kong-admin --url)/apis/ \
 --data 'name=movies' \
 --data 'hosts=cinema.com' \
 --data 'uris=/movies' \
 --data 'upstream_url=http://movies:5000'
```

Let's check whether it works correctly with the upstream_url.

```
curl -X GET $(minikube service kong-proxy --url)/movies \
  --header 'Host: cinema.com'

{
    "subresource_uris": {
        "movie": "/movies/<id>",
        "movies": "/movies"
    },
    "uri": "/"
}
```

Congratulations! We've just created the first API with Kong in a Kubernetes environment!

Monitor & analysis

Downtime with the API will have a far-reaching impact on your business. Users will drop from your service and due to uncomfortable experiences, your service reputation might take a loss. In this situation, solving the service defect is a time-critical job and without any visibility to APIs, diagnosing and solving the issue might take a long time. By monitoring the API in real time, the issues surface to the top and can be easily taken care of. This not only resolves the problem, but by analyzing the service log, you can prevent, identify, and solve the error before it breaks out.

Due to Kong API Management, logging becomes much easier. Without using it, users have to add a logging module to each service and monitor them separately to check their status. However, by putting Kong in front of each service, users only have to monitor this single entry point. It can collect all of the traffic to your services, so you only have to care about Kong.

In this section, we'll find out how to monitor Kong in real time and how to visualize and analyze with these logs.

Datadog (not open source)

Datadog is a monitoring and analytics service for cloud applications. By collecting all of the metrics from servers, databases, tools, and services, it provides real-time visibility of your entire stack with a unified view. Datadog suggests powerful monitoring & analytics services with various integrations. For a full list of integrations go **here**.

Datadog provides a 14 day free trial for new users with as many servers as you want. Or if you're a student, with **`Github Student pack`** you can claim two years of a free Pro Account for **`Datadog Student pack`**.

In this section, we'll look over monitoring Kong with datadog.
Here, we'll use the latest version of datadog agent `v5.21.2`.

INSTALLATION

To monitor Kong, you need to install `Datadog Agent` first. Replace <API_KEY> with your datadog **`API Key`**.

Installation is available in various distro/OS: **`Agent Installation`**.

```
 # Linux (Debain / Redhat)
export DD_API_KEY=<API_KEY>;
bash -c "$(curl -L https://raw.githubusercontent.com/
DataDog/dd-agent/master/packaging/datadog-agent/source/
install_agent.sh)"
```

CONFIGURATION

After installing it, you need to create a configuration file for Kong.
In the Datadog Agent's `conf.d` directory (`/etc/dd-agent/conf.d`), copy `kong.yaml.example` and configure it with your Kong instance.

```
init_config:

instances:
  - kong_status_url: http://localhost:8001/status/
```

```
  # For every instance, you need an `kong_status_url` and
can optionally supply a list of tags.
```

After configuring, restart the agent to send Kong metrics to Datadog. To validate your config, run `info` command with datadog-agent. It'll show you result of Kong configuration on **Checks** section.

```
sudo /etc/init.d/datadog-agent restart

  [ ok ] Restarting datadog-agent (via systemctl): datadog-
agent.service.

sudo /etc/init.d/datadog-agent info

  Checks
  ======
    kong
    -------
      - instance #0 [OK]
      - Collected 26 metrics, 0 events & 1 service check
```

By configuring the Datadog agent, metrics from `\status` of the Kong admin API will flow to Datadog. But to collect the full list of metrics with Kong, you need to configure the **`Kong Datadog Plugin`**.

```
curl -X POST http://localhost:8001/apis/{api}/plugins \
    --data "name=datadog" \
    --data "config.host=127.0.0.1" \
    --data "config.port=8125"
```

This will collect metrics from each API, such as `request.count`, `http_status_code`, `latency`, etc.

SETTING UP DASHBOARD

To visualize your metrics, you can use datadog's pre-set Kong dashboard or create your own Datadog dashboard.

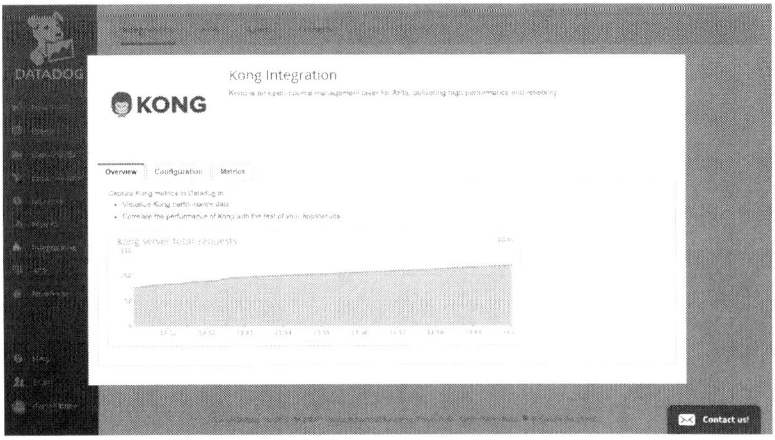

From the `Integrations` tab on Datadog, search Kong. By enabling `kong integration`, the pre-setted Kong `dashboard` will show up in your dashboard.

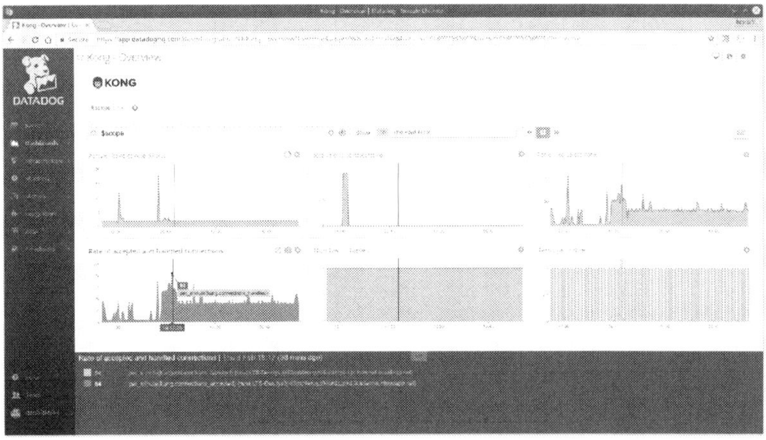

Also, you can customize the dashboard with each API's collected metric. Through this, you can visualize your API usage and analyze your API.

ELK Stack

ELK is the acronym for three open source projects:

- Elasticsearch: An open source, distributed, RESTful, JSON-based search engine.
- Logstash: Data processing pipeline that ingests data from multiple sources and sends it to Elasticsearch.
- Kibana: Visualize data with charts and graphs in Elasticsearch.

The basic workflow of ELK stack is this:

1. Users can collect their log (eg. service, DB, infrastructure) with `logstash` and send it to `elasticsearch`.
2. With this collected data; users can search and analyze specific data with `elasticsearch`.
3. Kibana as a visualization tool; users can visualize their data and monitor them in real time.

INSTALLATION

Here, we'll just skip everything related to `X-pack`, since explaining it will be out of the boundary of `Monitor & Analysis` for Kong.
More details about installing with full functionality of the ELK Stack is **here**.

Since `elasticsearch` works as the hub of this stack, we have to install it first.

```
wget -qO - https://artifacts.elastic.co/GPG-KEY-
elasticsearch | sudo apt-key add -
sudo apt-get install apt-transport-https
echo "deb https://artifacts.elastic.co/packages/6.x/apt
stable main" | sudo tee -a /etc/apt/sources.list.d/
elastic-6.x.list
sudo apt-get update && sudo apt-get install elasticsearch
```

Installing `elasticsearch` doesn't make itself run, so we have to enable and start it:

```
sudo systemctl daemon-reload
sudo systemctl enable elasticsearch.service
sudo systemctl start elasticsearch.service
```

To verify it's running correctly, issue the below command:

```
curl localhost:9200

{
  "name" : "TXEVdGI",
  "cluster_name" : "elasticsearch",
...... output truncated ......
  "tagline" : "You Know, for Search"
}
```

`Elasticsearch` is running properly! Next step is for `Kibana`, the visualization tool.

```
sudo apt-get install kibana
```

Also installing `kibana` doesn't make itself run, so we have to enable and start it:

```
sudo systemctl daemon-reload
sudo systemctl enable kibana.service
sudo systemctl start kibana.service
```

To verify it's running correctly, type `localhost:5601` in your browser.

If you are not running Kibana in your host, you can port foward to access the remote host's port.
ex) `ssh <kibana_host> -L 5601:localhost:5601`
Details about port fowarding are **here**.

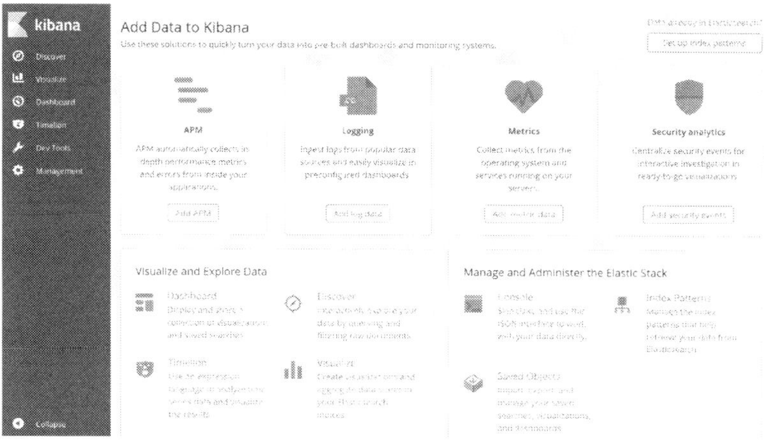

Lastly, for collecting data from remote services, install `logstash`.

```
sudo apt-get install logstash
```

Installing `logstash` doesn't make itself run, so we have to enable and start it:

```
sudo systemctl daemon-reload
sudo systemctl enable logstash.service
sudo systemctl start logstash.service
```

We'll skip verifying the `logstash` running status since it must be configured before running it.

You can check its status with `systemd`.

```
sudo systemctl status logstash.service
```

CONFIGURATION

To start collecting data, we need to create a pipeline for `logstash`. By default, `logstash` reads configuration files from the `conf.d` folder located in `logstash` home folder `/etc/logstash`.

Create a file with the name `kong.conf` in `/etc/logstash/conf.d` and fill it like below.

```
 # kong.conf
input {
  tcp {
```

```
    port => 12345
    codec => json
  }
}
filter {
  date {
    match => [ "timeMillis", "UNIX_MS" ]
  }
}
output {
  elasticsearch { hosts => ["localhost:9200"] }
  stdout { codec => rubydebug }
}
```

This configuration will make `logstash` work in this sequence:

1. Listen to TCP requests on port `12345` and parse it with the `json` format
2. With its input, modify or format with the `filter` section, which here is the `timestamp` format.
3. Lastly, send results data to `elasticsearch`, which is located at `localhost:9200`.
   And print the status of `logstash` to `stdout` output with `rubydebug` format.

We've just configured `logstash`, so let's restart it to work correctly.

```
sudo systemctl restart logstash.service
```

And now its time to configure Kong. To send Kong logs to `logstash`, we need to configure Kong with the TCP/UDP Plugin. Since we've configured `logstash` to collect data from the `TCP` request, we'll add the `TCP logging` plugin here.

```
curl -X POST http://localhost:8001/plugins \
    --data "name=tcp-log" \
    --data "config.host=localhost" \
    --data "config.port=12345"

{
   "created_at":1518266093000,
   "config":{
      "host":"localhost",
      "port":12345,
      "timeout":10000,
      "keepalive":60000,
```

```
        "tls":false
    },
    "id":"2a984c58-dbc8-4c35-a813-516158437c06",
    "enabled":true,
    "name":"tcp-log"
}
```

SETTING UP DASHBOARD

To monitor and analyze the logs from Kong, we have to look up `elasticsearch` for our data with using Kibana.
In order to visualize and monitor data in kibana, we need to create an index pattern to retrieve data from `elasticsearch`.

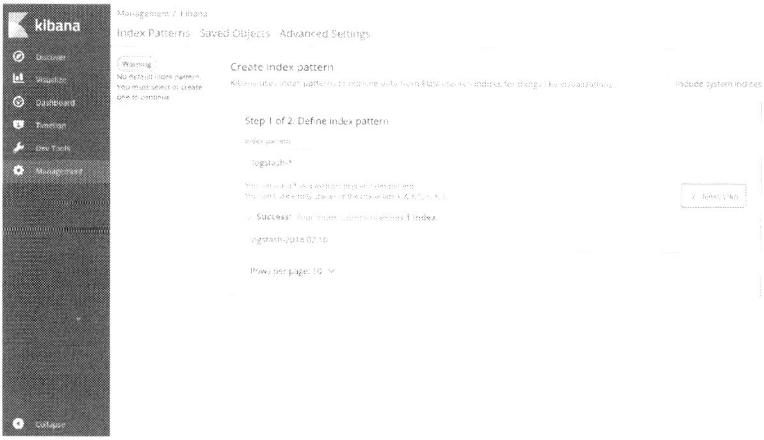

By typing the right index pattern (in here: `logstash-*`) and time filter, you can lookup your data in the `Discover` tab in kibana.

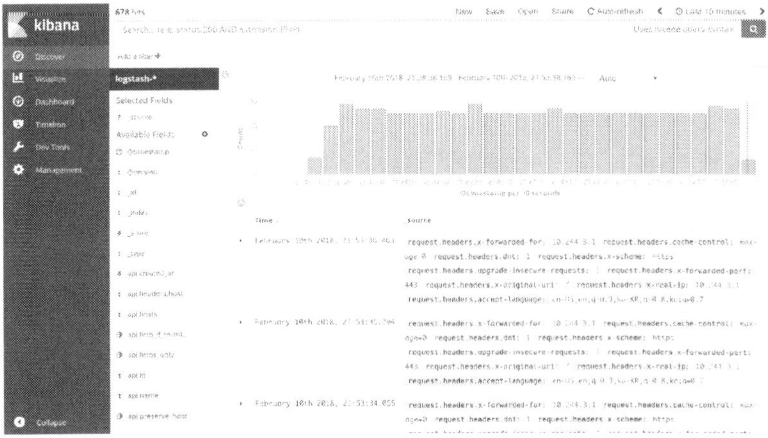

And with the collected data, you can visualize data with chats, table, maps, etc.

Configuration

Configuring Kong through the command line is a pretty tough job.

For example, let's say you are adding a new API. You have to look up Kong documentation for properly required attributes. And next, you have to type it on the command line while paying attention not to misspell any of the words.

Preparing all of the parameters with the appropriate attribute or headers takes time and a typo with the command will cause you to retype it again. To keep configuration simple, there are some open source integrations to help you with it. There are lists of options for this, such as 'Konga', 'Kong-Dashboard', 'KongDash', etc., but they basically do the same thing.

In this section, we'll only look at 'Konga,' which has richer functionalities than other integrations.

Konga

The description of **Konga** on the Github repository is: More than just another GUI to KONG Admin API.

This helps you with configuring Kong Admin API through the GUI dashboard, and it has much richer functionalities.

- Backup, restore and migrate Kong Nodes using Snapshots.
- Monitor Node and API states using health checks.
- Email/Application notifications.†
- Multiple users.

(from the official repository of Konga)

†: Slack Notification

INSTALLATION

For prerequisites for installation needs:

- A running Kong instance
- NodeJS / NPM

If you are prepared for prerequisites, installation for Konga is pretty simple.

```
git clone https://github.com/pantsel/konga.git
cd konga
npm install
```

Or you can run Konga with Docker.

```
docker run -p 1337:1337
  --link kong:kong
  --name konga
  pantsel/konga
```

To verify it's running correctly, open a browser and type `http://localhost:1337`. If you succeed with installing, you'll see a login page for Konga GUI.

The default password for Login is:

- Admin login: admin | password: adminadminadmin
- Demo user login: demo | password: demodemodemo

After login succeeds, you'll see a Welcome message with Kong Admin configuration.

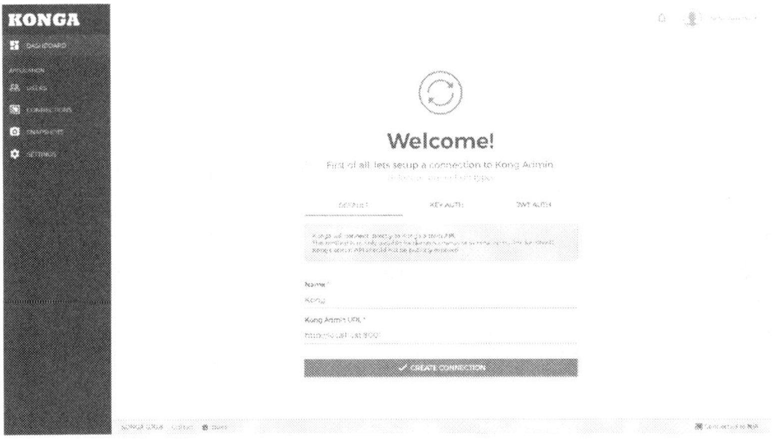

Fill in the form to configure with your own Kong Admin URL.

CONFIGURE KONG

Putting the right Kong Admin URL and creating a connection will show you the main dashboard that describes the status of your Kong node. It provides you with the information throughout the Kong nodes that can be accessed through http://<Kong_Admin_URL>/status.

Now we can add our API through this GUI dashboard. By clicking the API tab and `Add New API` button, you'll see a form with a bunch of hints for the parameters to be filled in with.

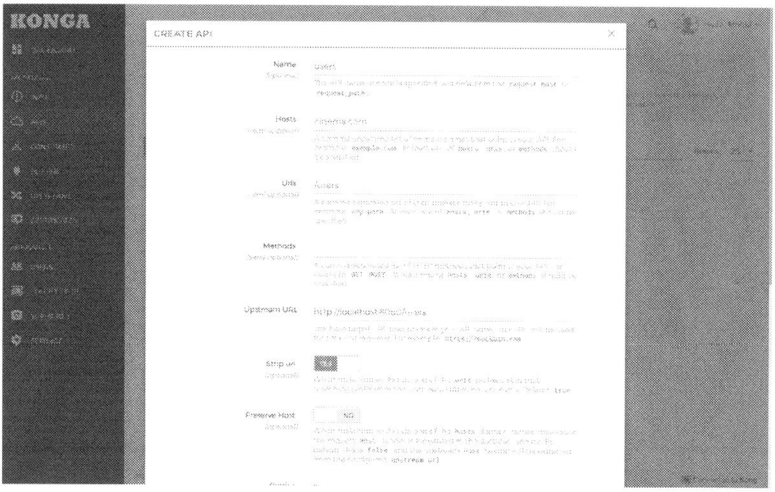

By clicking `Submit API`, you've just created your own API without typing any parameters or headers on the terminal. Konga does all the configuration stuff and sends it to the Admin API for you.

To add a plugin for your API, click `Add Plugin` on your API's Plugins tab. You can choose from the plugin list and easily add one of them to your API.

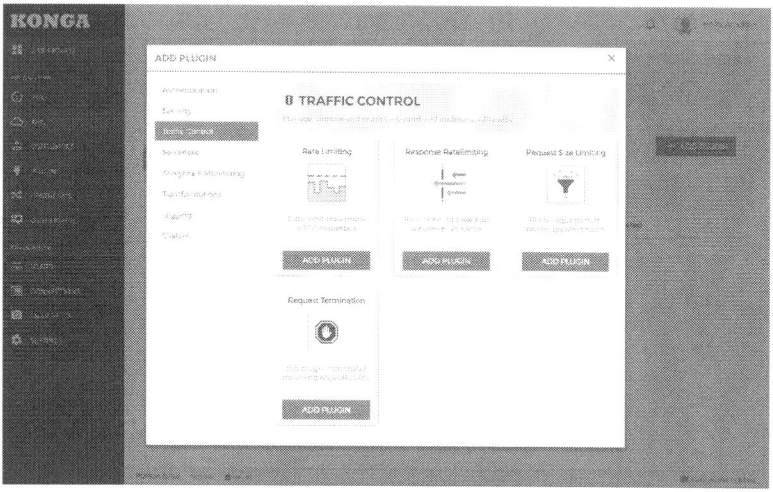

Also for the consumer, you can easily add new consumer and configure credential, ACL, APIs or etc.

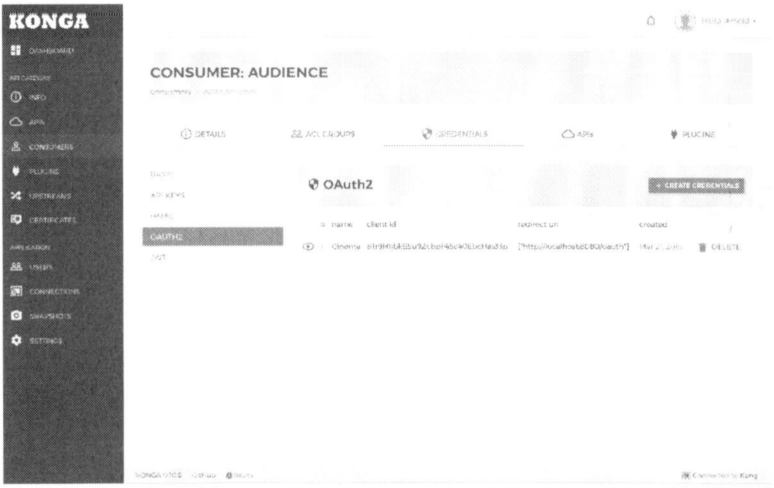

ADDITIONAL FUNCTIONALITIES

- Snapshot

Without using any integration, to backup your Kong settings, you have to access your datastore and create a dump file for that database. If your database is used for multipurpose and complexly configured, it'll be hard to backup your settings. Or if you are using different datastores (Cassandra, Postgresql) for each Kong nodes, due to two datastores aren't compatible with each other, the backup will be a tough process.

Konga's snapshot function can easily help you with this by abstracting datastore. It has own persistence mechanism for storing users and configuration, and by this users can backup, restore and migrate Kong Nodes easily.

By clicking `Instant Snapshot` from the snapshot tab, backup for Kong node is created with a short amount of time.

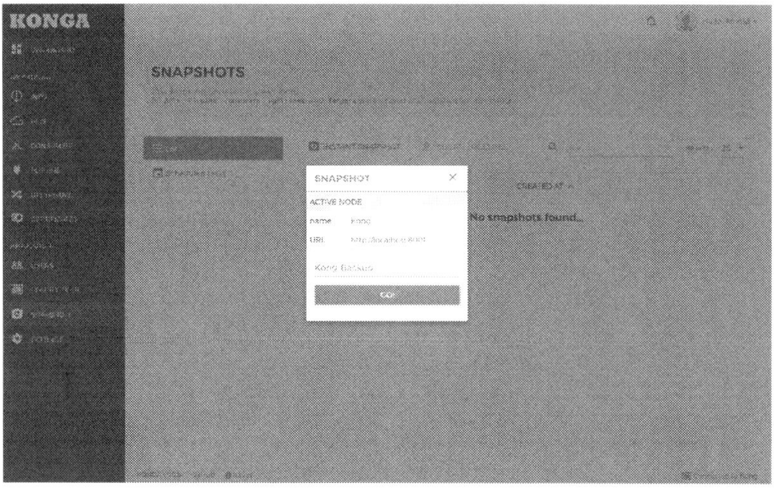

On each snapshot, you can check each category (API, Plugin, Consumer) details and choose which one to restore or export.

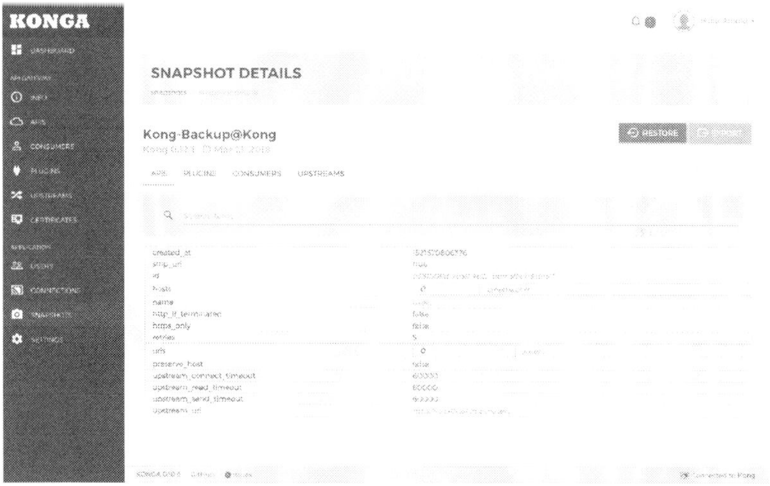

- Notification

When service is in operation, your server must stay healthy. Any incidents must be dealt with in a short amount of time. To be informed about your resources status, Konga can help you with health notifications.

If your Kong node is down, or one of your APIs is not responding, Konga will send you email or an application notification.

After configuring the health check for Node or API, notifications will be sent according to the `Notification` section from the settings tab.

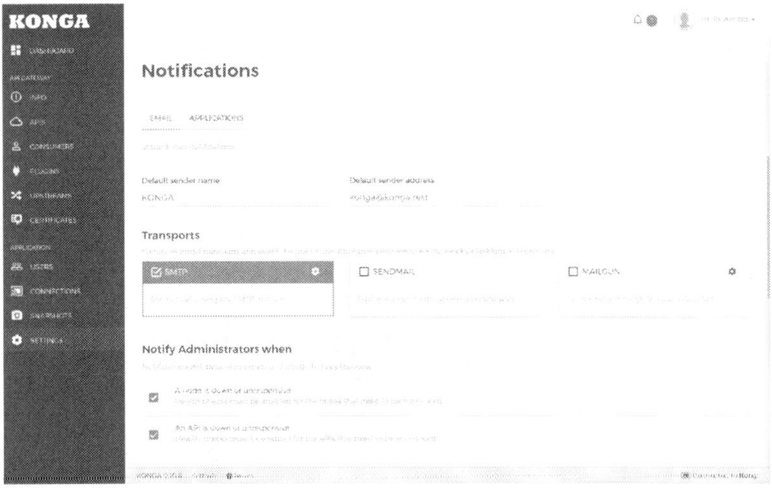

If you are using Slack with your team, by adding the Slack webhook URL on Konga, your team can be notified of the health status.

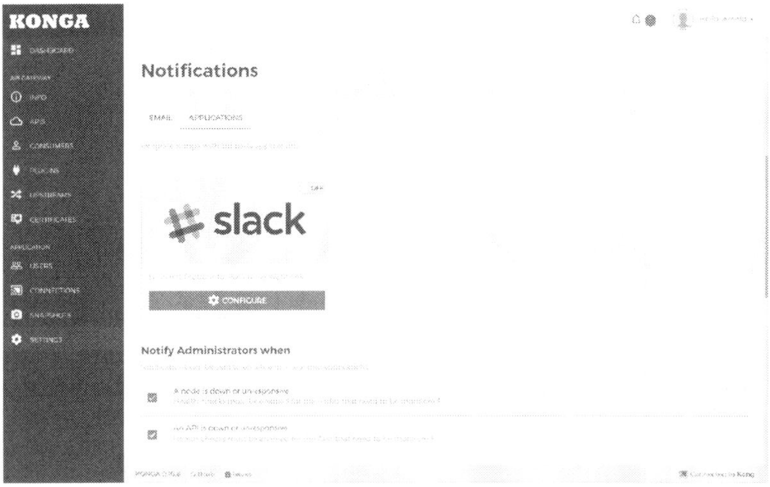

Summary

You are now prepared to use Kong with Docker and Kubernetes and other tools that make it easier to run and monitor Kong.

8 API Gateway Techniques

The API Gateway is a component of API Management.

API Management takes a bigger scope than API Gateway, which means API Management is the whole process of generating and publishing APIs, while API Gateway is more like an API interface or middleware. In practice, the API Gateway works as a connector between services that are responsible to receive requests, pass them to the backend service and give a response back to consumers. Hence, the API Gateway must be able to be identified. It is also mean to be as efficient as possible to work effectively.

All of the code for the sample project in this book can be found **here**.

Multi Consumer management

As written in Chapter 3, one of the API Gateway uses is to control traffic. API Traffic depends on how many consumers and how many requests per each consumer. It is important to differentiate which consumer is prohibited to access your APIs, and what consumer can access that. Back to the cinema system example. Let's say there are two third-party interfaces for a payment gateway; from bank A and bank B. Bank A can only update the transactions status of their customers that use their services, and the same with bank B. It will be troublesome if bank A is able to update transaction statuses of customers from bank B.

Versioning management

The consumers of an API will invest a significant amount of time and resources building client applications. It is important to guarantee that the API will provide its service for a long period of time without breaking the commitments undertaken with the consumer organizations. If an API is modified while client applications are using the old version, it must be verified beforehand so the new features will be able to coexist with the existing functionality.

In terms of the API Gateway itself, the benefit of using versioning is to help your system to be upgraded smoothly. Take an example of your Android native app. You have released version 2.0.0, where there is a payment feature. Then you upgraded your app having version 2.1.0 that provides push notifications about payment statuses. Say that your version 2.1.0 does not work in Android kit-kat below. If you differentiate your consumers based on versions there won't be any problems about unnecessary data for Android kit-kat or previous versions of Android. You can always send data based on consumers' need.

The next paragraphs detail which types of changes are backward compatible, which numbering conventions apply, and how to make Kong handle several versions of an API on the same server.

CHANGES THAT MAINTAIN BACKWARD COMPATIBILITY

The following changes on an API are backward compatible:

- Add a resource (path) or a verb (operation) to an API.
- Add optional input fields (query or path parameters, headers) to existing operations.
- Convert an input parameter from mandatory to optional.
- Add a new output parameter in the response.

CHANGES THAT BREAK BACKWARD COMPATIBILITY

These changes will break backward compatibility:

- Remove resources (path) or verbs (operations).
- Add mandatory input fields.
- Convert input fields from optional to mandatory.
- Modify the name or the type of a parameter.
- Add pagination support to a query that returns multiple objects. This will effect existing client applications, because these applications will not be aware that a query is now returning only a page of the results and not the complete result set.

MAJOR, MINOR AND FIX VERSIONS

Typically an API version will be identified with three numbers separated by a dot: MAJOR.MINOR.PATCH. The following rules explain when a new version of an API should be marked as a MAJOR change, a MINOR change, or just a PATCH:

- MAJOR. A new MAJOR version will be used when a new release includes incompatible changes to the API.
- MINOR. A new MINOR version will be used when new features are included to the API and these changes are backward compatible.
- PATCH. A new PATCH version will be used when just some bug fixes are done in the API, obviously maintaining the backward compatibility.

SUPPORTING SEVERAL VERSIONS ON THE SAME GATEWAY

Currently, Kong supports the existence of different versions of an API, provided that the version number is included in the URL:

- Requests to **http://localhost:8000/v1/movies** send the request to the microservice that implements the v1 of the functionality.
- Requests to **http://localhost:8000/v2/movies** send the request to v2.

Logging for failure or error

API Gateway allows us to store logs of requests and responses using various transports, like TCP, UDP, HTTP, and others. Log files help analyze traffic and make it easier to trace errors or fails inside the whole system. Logging for failure or error handling in the Gateway level must be done carefully, since it comes from various services and consumers.

CLEAR DATA ORIGIN

It is important to know which services or consumers produced errors or failures. The sequences will be:

- Which service or consumer
- When it happens
- Which event it is
- Who triggered the event (authorized user if any)
- What is the processed data (both input and output)

- What is the expected input / output

Both services and consumers have to store local log files. It helps developers trace whether error or failures happen at the gateway level, in the services level, or even at the consumers level.

NOTIFICATIONS FOR FAILURES OR ERRORS

Besides the activity of storing local errors log, being alert about failure or error before your customer finds out is an important task. There are several plugins for traffic alerts in Kong that can be used, like Runscope for HTTP request or response.

Caching criteria

The caching process happens in-memory because there is a need to avoid querying the datastore every time. But not all requests can be cached. For example, there are available movies. Imagine your customers see the "Kong: Micro Island" movie showing at 11:45, with one available seat for her. She tries to buy a ticket, but a pop up message appears saying, "There is no seat available," while the movies list shows that there is an available seat. This won't be a nice experience for customers. The criteria of caching must be:

- Time based expired. This an be used to cache the data that does not frequently change, like casts, titles, or synopsis
- Data frequency. This can be used for data that frequently changes, but is also frequently accessed, like ratings.

Rate limiting

Providing an API Gateway for various consumers means that your API Gateway should be available and reliable in any circumstance. There are scenarios that might happen in the API Gateway usage:

- Infinite requests from one consumer within a second that caused the API Gateway to be too busy to handle other requests.
- You need to keep it fair between high priority requests and low priority requests.

Rate limiting helps cover both scenarios in many ways.

LIMIT THE AMOUNT OF REQUESTS CONSUMERS MAY HAVE

In order to protect the API Gateway from bottlenecks, it is better to prevent the requests from being made from one consumer. Here, you can set the number of allowed requests based on a period of time. It is better to decrease the number of potential unused requests. In your responsive web app, where showtime lists displayed on the frontpage and also the most frequent accessed page, you can set 60 requests per second. As for movie details, you can set 30 requests per second, as it is accessed less often.

ALLOCATE MORE FOR HIGHER PRIORITY REQUESTS

Which is more fatal, terminating transactions and leaving incomplete payments, or asking customer to reload their homepage?

Always put finance transactions as a higher priority than displaying processes. It is better to ask customers to reload their homepage instead of leaving an incomplete finance transaction. There is the option of using Redis or cluster. But once again you have to wisely choose which data should be using Redis or cluster since it is done in-memory.

Routing common issues

To keep your services dependent, can you do a nested API Gateway?

The answer should be an easy no. But you often fail in this option and make the API Gateway do requests for itself. The reason for not doing nested requests is the potential of an infinite loop if you don't carefully map a request path. On the other hand, you left your API Gateway dependent on itself for results.

HTTP CORS issues

If your API Gateway makes an HTTP request to a different domain, it needs to be CORS-friendly. If you use cross domain requests, you need to add the Access-Control-Allow-Origin header to your responses in your handlers. If you're using cookies or other authentication, you'll also need to add the Access-Control-Allow-Credentials header to your response. But no worries, Kong has a CORS plugin so you don't have to manually do this.

Specific-Purpose route

Is it okay to have two routes for one request in a different scenario? For example, you may have a route to display showtime lists that display price in the Euro and another route to display showtime lists that display price in USD.

If you do routes like that, it is the same as putting business logic in the frontend level. Which means, both the native Android app and responsive web app should have known where to call and when. Both of them have to detect which nationality belongs to a customer and which route should be called.

POST OR GET NOT ANY FOR HTTP REQUESTS

The basic HTTP methods for REST APIs, with no ambiguity, will be helpful for data logging. Here are those methods:

- GET—For returning resources
- POST—For creating a new resource
- PUT—For replacing a resource
- PATCH—For updating a resource with versions
- DELETE—For deleting a resource

Business authorization in the API Gateway

The API Gateway may authenticate the user. But this does not mean it can always authorize users. What if a blacklist user can't book a movie show, but can see a movie showtime? Should it be authorized in the Gateway level? A user's scope can be very specific and it can change the core of the system. It is better to put a user's authorization, especially business authorization for a user in the level of services. There are several options of access tokens that can be passed to services from the API Gateway like OAuth2. Chapter 10 will describe this.

Composing data in the API Gateway

In order to make responses more consumer-oriented, use transformers. Your scenarios of using a transformer might be similar to these:

1. Collaborating two or more services respond in a single request

2. Remove, rename, replace, add, or even append a request and/or response

Let's say your native Android app runs in a medium screen size capable of displaying information of movie showtimes and details like casts and ratings. And say you construct your services like this:

1. Showtime services

ID	TITLE	SHOW-TIME	PRICE	Short Desc
MV-1709-001	Kong: Micro Island	12:45	$10	...
MV-1709-001	Alien: Components	13:45	$10	...
MV-1709-003	King Artie: Legend of the Swarm	21:15	$10	...

1. Movie services

ID	TITLE	CASTS	RAT-INGS	RELEASE DATE
MV-1709-001	Kong: Micro Island	Brit, Tim, Sam	8	2017-09-01
MV-1709-001	Alien: Components	Ailee, Dave	7	2017-09-01
MV-1709-003	King Artie: Legend of the Swarm	Cliff, Joan	8	2017-09-01

Your Native Android app needs data like this:

ID	TITLE	SHOW-TIME	PRICE	CASTS	RAT-INGS
MV-1709-001	Kong: Micro Island	12:45	$10	Brit, Tim, Sam	8
MV-1709-001	Alien: Components	13:45	$10	Ailee, Dave	7
MV-1709-003	King Artie: Legend of the Swarm	21:15	$10	Cliff, Joan	8

To have results like in the table above, you need to join your showtime services and movie services based on a movie ID. It can be done in the Gateway level. As you know, most of the logical functions in the Gateway level were done in-memory. Again, it costs more for the API Gateway. Besides, the API Gateway must be smart enough to handle unstructured data since the microservices architecture allows us to have various databases, like mongoDB, mySQL, Cassandra and others. The other option is applying the Command Query Responsibility Segregation (CQRS) pattern to do the composing.

Transforming API requests and responses

Let's say you applied the CQRS Pattern and have read-only data like this:

ID	TITLE	SHOWTIME	PRICE	CASTS	RATINGS
MV-1709-001	Kong: Micro Island	12:45	$10	Brit, Tim, Sam	8
MV-1709-001	Alien: Components	13:45	$10	Ailee, Dave	7
MV-1709-003	King Artie: Legend of the Swarm	21:15	$10	Cliff, Joan	8

At the same time your cinema system is scaling up, allowing a display price based on users' nationality, your app is available for smaller screen size so that there is no need to display ratings and casts.

ID	TITLE	SHOWTIME	PRICE
MV-1709-001	Kong: Micro Island	12:45	€8.06
MV-1709-001	Alien: Components	13:45	€8.06
MV-1709-003	King Artie: Legend of the Swarm	21:15	€8.06

Modifying responses for specific purposes are better done in the services level, since handling policies in the Gateway level could mess up the application design. Besides, you have to change all consumers' settings if the policies have changed.

Although microservices allow every service to be deployed independently, it will be difficult if each service has a different terminology of similar things, such as pagination. For example, your showtime services with pagination may use `skip` and `take` as parameters, while your movie services use parameters like `page` and `take`. Then your API Gateway has to translate consumer's parameters so they can be understood by services.

Doing workflow in the API Gateway

Let's say you have a flow like this:

1. Customer books two tickets for watching a movie in a booking service
2. Service generates an invoice in the billing service
3. System sends an invoice to email using a third-party mail service

It is common to have relationships between processes of different services like this sample above. But, it is better not to do it in the Gateway level. Despite the memory usage issue, it causes high dependencies between services in the Gateway level, and risks too much if one of the flows fails. Doing this in the Gateway level is much more like doing monolith scenarios in the Gateway level. There are options to do event driven processes in a microservices way that use a message broker.

Summary

You should now have a deeper understanding of the API Gateway for Kong and how to best use it. In the next chapter we'll focus on API security.

API Security 9

In a microservices architecture, the API Gateway acts as a security endpoint. It is crucial to protect the access to those microservices so only authorized applications, usually referred to as *clients*, are able to interact with those services. It is required to provide to end users, or *resource owners*, a mechanism to protect their valuable data from unwanted access.

During the last few years, the banking industry has invested a lot of time and resources to create and expose APIs. There are several initiatives, such as the CMA's Open Banking in the UK, or the Payments Service Directive 2 (PSD2) in the European Union, that are pushing banks to securely expose their customer's information using APIs. The mechanisms used to protect those APIs will be explained in this chapter.

Kong provides several plugins that can be used to protect APIs. In the next sections, we cover how to use those plugins to add a strong security layer on top of the microservices.

All of the code for the sample project in this book can be found **here**.

Key authentication

It is common that only a set of identified client applications will be allowed to interact with APIs exposed on Kong. If a bank uses Kong to expose a Payments API, the bank will probably use an on-boarding process to identify which third-parties want to use that Payments API on their applications. Some examples of such third-parties are retailers, small FinTech companies, etc. That on-boarding process will have several steps, including online forms, that will be used to ask the third-party what type of application it is planning to write. The on-boarding process will most likely include offline and back office steps, such as asking those companies to sign documents like contracts or a code of ethics agreement.

Finally, as the last step of that process, the bank will provide to the third-party a secret key that will be used to interact with the API. That key will only identify the client application, but not to the resource owner. To protect the information of the resource owner, a different mechanism called OAuth2 will be used, which is covered next.

Another interesting use of API keys is for analytics and billing purposes. One of the main benefits of an API Management tool is that it provides a convenient way to detect if an API is being used very often, or on the other hand, if it is becoming obsolete because its usage is declining. That tracking can be done on a consumer-by-consumer basis. You can create reports filtered by consumers using their API key to detect exactly what is the historical usage of an API by a particular customer. If there is a contract in which the usage of that API is being billed monthly, the use of the API key is crucial in order to be able to determine how many API calls the customer has completed in a specific period of time.

Creating consumers

Once the company has identified who the third-parties are that want to consume the API, those third-parties must be added to the database of Kong, as Consumers. That operation will be done using Kong's Admin API, interacting with the resource Consumer.

In Chapter 5, "Meet the Kong," some verbs associated with Consumer were shown. This table adds more verbs associated with API Security (OAuth2, JWT and API Keys):

Verb	Path	Description
GET	/consumers/{username or id}/oauth2	List the client applications belonging to that consumer. Those applications will have a client_id and a client_secret.
POST	/consumers/{username or id}/oauth2	Creates a new Application for a consumer. During the creation of the application, a redirect URI is specified, which will be useful in some OAuth flows.
GET	/consumers/{username or id}/key-auth	Lists the API keys a Consumer has.
POST	/consumers/{username or id}/key-auth	Creates a new API key for this Consumer.

Verb	Path	Description
GET	/consumers/{user-name or id}/jwt	Lists the credentials associated to this Consumer that will be used to validate JWT.
POST	/consumers/{user-name or id}/jwt	Creates new credentials for this Consumer to validate JWT.

The first step to create a Consumer is to POST a new resource to the collection Consumers, as it was explained in Chapter 5. For example, the following curl command will be used to create a new Consumer called `PurpleMall`:

```
$ curl -X POST http://localhost:8001/consumers/ --data
"username=PurpleMall"
```

Kong will return an *HTTP 201 Created* in case the operation was successful, with this JSON object as a response:

```
{
    "created_at":1517083052000,
    "username":"PurpleMall",
    "id":"3f3d9926-349c-4bb2-b378-9b6a6f40a1cb"
}
```

It is possible to check if the Consumer was created by using a GET operation to retrieve the collection of Consumers:

```
$ curl -X GET http://localhost:8001/consumers/
```

That operation will return this collection. The ID of the consumer, or alternatively the name, will be used later to create an API key for that customer:

```
{
    "total": 1,
    "data": [
        {
            "created_at":1517083052000,
            "username":"PurpleMall",
            "id":"3f3d9926-349c-4bb2-b378-9b6a6f40a1cb"
        }
    ]
}
```

If the API is going to be used by other third-parties, it is needed to create new Consumers by repeating the previous POST operation.

Protecting an API with the Key Authentication plugin

Once we have created at least one Consumer, the next step is to protect the API by using the *Key Authentication* plugin. The parameters of this plugin are:

Parameter	Type	Default	Description
config.key_names	Optional	apikey	It is an array of comma separated parameter names. The Key Authentication plugin will look at either headers or query parameters that match a name found in this list, to find a suitable key.
config.hide_credentials	Optional	false	It is a boolean. A value of true will hide to the microservices the key, so they will be unaware of the existence of this parameter.

There are more parameters such as config.key_in_body, config.anonymous or config.run_on_preflight. Please refer to the documentation of the plugin to learn more about those parameters.

Before activating the *Key Authentication* plugin, it is necessary to detect which ID of the API is going to be protected. That can be done by querying the APIs collection using this command:

```
$ curl -X GET http://localhost:8001/apis/
```

Alternatively, it is possible to use the name of the API, which probably is easier and more convenient. Assuming that the name of the API that is going to be protected is 'movies' this curl instruction will enable the *Key Authentication* plugin on that API:

```
$ curl -X POST http://localhost:8001/apis/movies/plugins \
    --data "name=key-auth" \
    --data "config.key_names=apikey"
```

The output of that instruction will be:

```
{
    "created_at":1517083831000,
    "config":
    {
        "key_names": ["apikey"],
        "key_in_body":false,
        "anonymous":"",
        "run_on_preflight":true,
        "hide_credentials":false
    },
    "id":"d8b5f6ff-9b25-4f84-8b5e-c7cc71548a2f",
    "name":"key-auth",
    "api_id":"bd5baf99-7838-46b7-a81f-575a3726c7b5",
    "enabled":true
}
```

Once a particular API has been configured to use the *Key Authentication* plugin, that API becomes unusable unless the client applications include a header named *apikey* with a valid value.

Assigning keys to client applications

Once the plugin is enabled, the next step is to create a key for the consumer. Other API Management tools usually provide a pair of keys: an *apikey* and an *apisecret*. In case the API Management tool supports it, it is usually a good practice to use a pair of keys instead of just one. Later on in the OAuth2 section it will be shown that usually, most OAuth2 flows depend on the existence of a client_id and optionally a client_secret.

The API key is associated with a Consumer. Using the ID of the Consumer created previously (or the name of the Consumer), the following curl will create a new API key (the trailing -d parameter is needed, in order to guarantee that the body of the request is empty):

```
curl -X POST http://localhost:8001/consumers/
3f3d9926-349c-4bb2-b378-9b6a6f40a1cb/key-auth -d ''
```

The output of that command is:

```
{
    "id":"9a5fa2b0-d6dd-476a-9d61-0d55a9c7c6ff",
    "created_at":1517087501000,
    "key":"bP0MSdFkkUNz4NQQNzVw2iQ25c3XbotN",
    "consumer_id":"3f3d9926-349c-4bb2-b378-9b6a6f40a1cb"
}
```

The most important part of the output of that command is the *key* field. That information must be sent to the third-party using any safe mechanism. It is not recommended to use email to exchange keys; most high-end API Management tools provide a Developer Portal that can be used as a self-service for Consumers to generate their own API keys on the fly.

Using a key to invoke an API

Once the Consumer has the API keys and the API has been configured with the Key Authentication plugin in order to interact with the API, it will need to pass an additional header named *apikey* with the value of the API key:

```
$ curl -X GET http://localhost:8000/movies -H 'apikey:
bP0MSdFkkUNz4NQQNzVw2iQ25c3XbotN'
```

If the header "apikey" is present, Kong will accept the request and return an appropriate answer. If the header is not present or the value is wrong, Kong will return an *HTTP 401 Unauthorized* error or an *HTTP 403 Forbidden* error.

Alternatively, it is possible to pass the *apikey* in the query string. However, it is not a recommended practice, because the query string usually contains parameters related to pagination, sorting, etc. Security parameters are expected to be found on headers.

Protecting APIs with OAuth2

API keys are a simple and convenient way to protect API usage from unsolicited applications and consumers. But, detecting if a client application is allowed or not to use an API is not enough. An authorization model is needed in which end users (the *resource owners*) will be able to allow or disallow a client application to get access to their personal data or to perform operations on behalf of them.

OAuth2 is an authorization standard commonly used to grant to websites or applications access to the resource owners information. The first version (OAuth) was released in 2010 (RFC 5849). Two years later, in 2012, a second version of the standard (OAuth2; RFC 6749) was released, making the first version of OAuth obsolete. In 2014, OpenID Connect was published, as an authentication layer on top of OAuth2.

Although most end users are unaware of the existence of OAuth2, the truth is that it is the protocol running behind the scenes whenever a user authorizes an application to log in using the Facebook or Linkedin credentials, or when those users allow another application to get access to their profile on those social networks. In that case, a concrete grant type of OAuth2 called *Authorization Code* is used to allow the end users to log in to a website using their Facebook or Linkedin credentials.

UK Open Banking relies on OAuth2 as its foundational framework for API Security. As OAuth2 is just an authorization framework, and not an authentication framework, Open Banking also recommends the use of OpenID Connect on top of OAuth2.

OAuth2 is used by resource owners to provide to client applications temporary access to their personal data. At the heart of the protocol, it is the creation of temporary *access tokens*, thus avoiding the need to provide the password to those client applications. A *token* may be seen like a temporary opaque ID that can be used by a third-party client application to retrieve information that belongs to a resource owner or to perform operations in the name of the resource owner.

There are four different ways to grant access to those client applications using OAuth2:

- Client Credentials grant
- Authorization Code grant
- Resource Owner Password Credentials grant
- Implicit grant

Additionally, the specification includes two other flows:

- Refresh token grant. It can be used to request a new access token when the previous one has expired.
- JWT Profile. Sets the value of grant_type as "urn:ietf:params:oauth:grant-type:jwt-bearer" and uses a JWT as assertion to obtain an OAuth2 Access Token.

Kong has plugins that implement OAuth2 and OpenID Connect. On the next sections, it will be explained how to use those plugins to implement the different OAuth2 grant types.

Enabling OAuth2 plugin

The *OAuth 2.0 Authentication* plugin has different parameters, summarized in this table:

Parameter	Type	Default	Description
name	Manda-tory		Must be *oauth2*
config.scopes	Optional		It is an array of scopes separated by commas. A scope is typically a permission, the specific detail of which type of data belonging to the resource owner the client application wants to read or write. It may be as well an operation, for example, the ability to make a payment using an account belonging to the resource owner.
config.to-ken_expira-tion	Optional	7200	The number of seconds this token will be valid. It is recommended to use very low values, for example just a couple of minutes. A value of 300 seconds will be acceptable. By using Refresh Tokens, the client application can extend the life of the token.
config. en-able_authori-zation_code	Optional	false	If enabled, the plugin of OAuth2 will be able to use the Authorization Code grant.
config. en-able_cli-ent_creden-tials	Optional	false	If enabled, the plugin of OAuth2 will be able to use the Client Credentials grant.
config. en-able_implic-it_grant	Optional	false	If enabled, the plugin of OAuth2 will be able to use the Implicit Grant.
config. en-able_pass-word_grant	Optional	false	If enabled, the plugin of OAuth2 will be able to use the Resource Owner Password Credentials grants.
config. hide_creden-tials	Optional	false	If enabled, Kong will remove the OAuth2 headers when invoking the underlying microservices. It is recommended to enable this parameter.
config. re-fresh_to-ken_ttl	Optional	1209600	The number of seconds the refresh token will be valid. It is recommended to think carefully about a proper value of this parameter in terms of business im-

Parameter	Type	Default	Description
			plications and security. A very low value (just a couple of days) will affect the user experience of the client applications (users will be asked too often to enter their credentials) and a value too high may have security implications.

There are more parameters such as config.mandatory_scope, config.auth_header_name, etc. Please, refer to the documentation of the plugin to learn more.

The following curl instruction could be used to protect an API called *movies* to use the authorization code grant, to set a lifetime of the tokens of 4 minutes (240 seconds), and to establish 'ratings' and 'revenue' as valid scopes:

```
$ curl -X POST http://localhost:8001/apis/movies/plugins \
    --data "name=oauth2" \
    --data "config.enable_authorization_code=true" \
    --data "config.token_expiration=240" \
    --data "config.scopes=ratings,revenue"
```

Once the plugin is enabled, a Provision Key will be created. That provision key will be used to interact with the OAuth2 endpoints of the API and is supposed to be secret, so only internal applications, usually login forms, will know its value.

As it was described in the section *Key Authentication*, it is necessary to create a Consumer to identify the third-party that will consume the API. That can be done by issuing a curl command like this:

```
$ curl -X POST http://localhost:8001/consumers/ --data
"username=DisruptiveFinTech"
```

A Consumer may have different applications consuming an API. So, for example, a FinTech company may have a Data Aggregation application (subscribed to the Accounts API of several banks) but it may have as well a Quick Payments applications (subscribed to the Payments API). Those applications will be associated with a Consumer using a curl command like this:

```
$ curl -X POST http://localhost:8001/consumers/
DisruptiveFinTech/oauth2 \
```

```
    --data "name=DataAggregation" \
    --data "redirect_uri=http://getkong.org"
```

The output of curl will be:


```
{
    "client_id":"jJGCzhxxEst50sOtywFOINSRvfh48dNB",
    "created_at":1517168275000,
    "id":"7ed353cd-a6ba-4d6c-9146-fb3c781e2ebe",
    "redirect_uri":["http:\/\/www.getkong.org"],
    "name":"DataAggregation",
    "client_secret":"AuIgB5NM4zU57EjHfP8su6bfA3EtnZny",
    "consumer_id":"fee36abc-2474-49b7-addd-7d6b56a16316"
}
```


That curl command is using the parameter *name* to set the name of the consuming application (in this case DataAggregation). The parameter *redirect_uri* is also set to establish the URL that will be used to redirect the browser of the users once they have entered their credentials on the login page of their bank and have allowed the FinTech company to access their data.

That curl command will generate as well a pair of keys (client_id and client_secret) that will be used to interact with the OAuth2 endpoints. In case the API is going to be consumed by third-parties, the values of those fields must be provided to those companies in a secure way (avoiding email).

Once the plugin is enabled on an API, two new resources will be available via POST for that API. Those endpoints must be accessed using HTTPS (for example, the port 8443) because it is a requirement of OAuth2:

- oauth2/authorize - Used to generate codes in the Authorization Code grant
- oauth2/token - Used to obtain access tokens, to refresh tokens, etc.

The parameters used to interact typically with oauth2/authorize are:

Parameter	Type	Description
client_id	Mandatory	The ID of the application that wants to obtain an access token.
response_type	Mandatory	The type of response of this endpoint. It will typically be 'code'.

Parameter	Type	Description
scope	Mandatory	It is an array of scopes separated by commas.
provision_key	Mandatory	The provision key created when the OAuth2 plugin was enabled for this API.
authenticated_userid	Mandatory	The user id of the resource owner.

The parameters used to interact typically with oauth2/token are:

Parameter	Type	Description
client_id	Mandatory	The ID of the application that wants to obtain an access token.
client_secret	Optional	The secret of the application that wants to obtain an access token.
grant_type	Mandatory	The type of grant: authorization_code, password, client_credentials, implicit or refresh_token.
scope	Mandatory	It is an array of scopes separated by commas.
provision_key	Optional	The provision key created when the OAuth2 plugin was enabled to this API.
authenticated_userid	Optional	The user id of the resource owner.
refresh_token	Optional	If grant_type is refresh_token, this parameter will hold the refresh token
code	Optional	If grant_type is authorization_code, this parameter will hold the code.

In the next sections, the different OAuth2 grant flows are explained.

Client Credentials grant

It is common in internal environments that a consuming application needs to interact with an API in order to retrieve static information such as the list of branches of a bank, the list of supply chain providers, the list of countries in which a company is operating, etc. In that case, that information is not associated with a particular resource owner, so it does not make any sense to interact with that API using the username and password of a particular customer or employee.

For these cases, it is very common to use a simplistic OAuth2 flow called *Client Credentials*. The credentials that will be used to obtain an OAuth2 access token will just be the ID of the client application. There is no need to involve any resource owner to provide their credentials, because this flow is intended to be used by consuming applications that just need to see general information or to perform operations not directly associated to a particular person.

This curl command will be used to enable the *OAuth 2.0 Authentication* plugin to use a Client Credentials flow on the Movies API:

```
$ curl -X POST http://localhost:8001/apis/movies/plugins \
    --data "name=oauth2" \
    --data "config.enable_client_credentials=true"
```

The Client Credentials is so simple that it does not even require the plugin to establish a set of known scopes.

As described in the previous section (Enabling OAuth2 plugin) after the plugin has been configured, it is required to execute two additional steps:

- Create a Consumer (POST **http://localhost:8001/consumers/**)
- Create an Application (POST POST **http://localhost:8001/consumers/{consumer_id}/oauth2**)

A consuming application will be able to obtain OAuth2 access tokens using this curl command (in this case, the SSL port 8443 is used). The parameters client_id an client_secret are obtained after creating an application for a particular Consumer:

```
$ curl -X POST https://localhost:8443/movies/oauth2/token \
    --data "client_id=fIeXHLeDwSuaCoHA0Bh2IgUeurBmX3Gt" \
    --data "client_secret=hhRrADE3XYjZp6DBU5ezRVpDt1gkkfK6" \
    --data "grant_type=client_credentials"
```

The response of curl will be:

```
{
    "token_type": "bearer",
    "access_token": "mzi3CJMautR8OTDWT5gwVKdWrGosSaCO",
    "expires_in": 7200
}
```

Sometimes it is needed to use the parameter -k in curl, in order to avoid SSL validation problems.

The access_token returned by curl can be used to interact with the Movies API, passing the token in an Authorization header:

```
curl -X GET http://localhost:8000/movies \
  -H 'Authorization: Bearer mzi3CJMautR8OTDWT5gwVKdWrGosSaCO'
```

If the Authorization header is missing, or the token is used after its expiration time, Kong will return an *HTTP 401 Unauthorized.*

Authorization Code grant

The Authorization Code is the most complex OAuth2 flow. It is commonly used when the client application that consumes an API maintained by a third-party and running in a separate infrastructure. Typically, a FinTech company will be using this OAuth2 flow to gain access to information of customers of banks, in a scenario like this:

- An end user (=resource owner) uses an application or website of a FinTech.
- At some point of the journey, the client application of the FinTech suggests the users to log in with the credentials of their banks. This may be useful, for example, to make a payment, or to analyze the transactions of an account.
- The browser is redirected to the login page of the bank and the user (=resource owner) is asked to provide the credentials.
- The resource owner logins to the bank. The resource owners are asked as well to confirm if they agree to let the FinTech company access the information associated with the scopes.
- The login form interacts with the oauth2/authorize endpoint to create a temporary code.
- The login form redirects the browser to a page that belongs to the FinTech website, passing a temporary code in the query string.
- The backend client application of the FinTech uses the temporary code to interact with the oauth2/token endpoint of the bank to obtain an access token and a refresh token.
- The client application uses the access token to temporarily consume APIs of the bank on behalf of the resource owner. When that access token expires, the FinTech uses the refresh token to obtain a new access token.

This diagram describes the Authorization code flow:

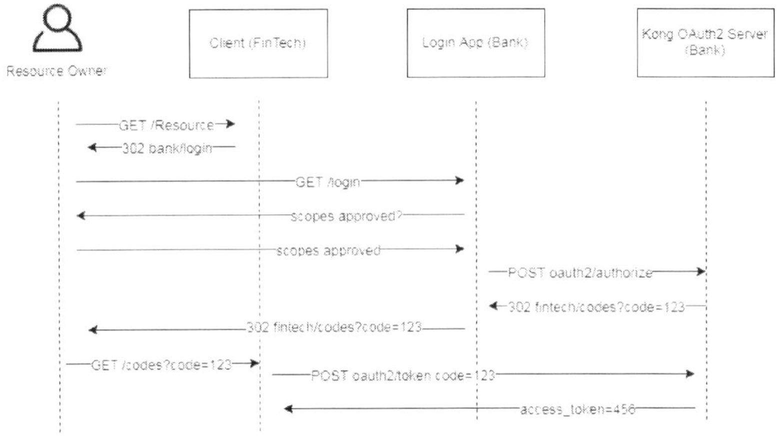

The first step to enable this OAuth2 flow with Kong is to configure the *OAuth 2.0 Authentication* plugin to use an Authorization Code flow. This curl command sets a couple of scopes (ratings and revenue), and instructs the OAuth2 server to require at least one scope accepted by the resource owner:

```
$ curl -X POST http://localhost:8001/apis/movies/plugins \
    --data "name=oauth2" \
    --data "config.scopes=ratings,revenue" \
    --data "config.mandatory_scope=true" \
    --data "config.enable_authorization_code=true"
```

The output of curl will include a provision_key that will be used later in a login form to be able to interact with the oauth2/authorize endpoint. As in any other OAuth2 flow, it is mandatory to perform two additional steps, as described in the "Enabling OAuth2 plugin" section:

- Create a Consumer (POST **http://localhost:8001/consumers/**)
- Create an Application (POST POST **http://localhost:8001/consumers/{consumer_id}/oauth2**). It is important to set a value for the parameter *redirect_uri* that links to a URL in the website of the third-party and that will be responsible to read the temporary code and exchange it with an OAuth2 access token using the oauth2/token endpoint.

To use the Authorization Code flow, you need:

- A login form running on the same infrastructure as Kong

- A form that asks the resource owner to grant access to the third-party to a set of scopes (this form is usually the same form as the login)
- A page on a website of the third-party website that can be accessed by the resource owner and that will contain the temporary authorization code.

In order to be able to test the grant, it is highly recommended to install any kind of mock login form that is able to simulate that the user is logged in, that the user has granted the scopes to the third-party, and that this third-party is getting the authorization code. Fortunately, in the GitHub repository of Kong there is a sample app (kong-oauth2-hello-world) that provides all of these artifacts. The steps required to install the kong-oauth2-hello-world are:

- Download the source code from GitHub
- Install the Node.js dependencies (npm install)
- Define required environment variables such as PROVISION_KEY, KONG_ADMIN and KONG_API URLs, the API_PATH of the API to be consumed, and a list of SCOPES.
- Run the app (node app.js)
- Use a browser to navigate to the URL of the app. That URL will include several query parameters, including the response_type (with a value of 'code'), some scopes, and the client_id created in the Consumer Application.

The sample app uses basically the oauth2/authorize endpoint to generate a temporary code. This is an illustrative example of the API call that the sample app *kong-oauth2-hello-world* is doing in its code:

```
$ curl -X POST https://localhost:8443/movies/oauth2/
authorize \
    --data "client_id=fIeXHLeDwSuaCoHA0Bh2IgUeurBmX3Gt" \
    --data "response_type=code" \
    --data "scope=ratings" \
    --data "provision_key=Nt1iqLe6CPN9Gv91L1nPDLlvzJgYZ5K2" \
    --data "authenticated_userid=userid123"
```

Once the app gets the authorization code, it will redirect to any mock URL. That URL will contain in the query string the temporary code. That code can be used to manually interact with the oauth2/token endpoint to get the access token:

```
$ curl -X POST https://localhost:8443/movies/oauth2/token \
    --data "client_id=fIeXHLeDwSuaCoHA0Bh2IgUeurBmX3Gt" \
```

```
    --data "client_secret=hhRrADE3XYjZp6DBU5ezRVpDt1gkkfK6" \
    --data "grant_type=authorization_code" \
    --data "code=GGp0UiTPVtpZbfme3bdaypzrUDLNTQln"
```

The output of curl will be:

```
{
    "refresh_token": "1XwV5uuzdaX6InOM7otIxKKVklOmDy5F",
    "token_type": "bearer",
    "access_token": "oNMSjPVAVCmQVSQqt2jESOrQ2eHHWKRB",
    "expires_in": 7200
}
```

Sometimes it is needed to use the parameter -k in curl, in order to avoid SSL certification problems.

That access_token can be used to interact with the Movies API, passing the token in an Authorization header:

```
curl -X GET http://locaslhost:8000/movies \
  -H 'Authorization: Bearer oNMSjPVAVCmQVSQqt2jESOrQ2eHHWKRB'
```

If the Authorization header is missing, or the token is used after its expiration time, Kong will return an *HTTP 401 Unauthorized*.

Resource Owner Password Credentials grant

There are some scenarios in which the client application has been created by the same organization that created the API. In that case, if both the client application and the API are running in the same infrastructure, it may be interesting if the client application uses its own login form to authenticate the user, so those credentials can be used as well to interact with the OAuth server directly, obtaining an access token.

This OAuth2 flow can be used if the following conditions are met:

- There is a relationship of trust between the consuming client application and the resource owner.
- The client application is able to obtain the user id and password of the user.
- The client application is able to validate the user id and password using, for example, an LDAP server.
- The client application and the API are running in the same organization.

This OAuth2 flow is commonly used as well in Single Sign-On scenarios. For example, it may be the case in which the consuming application has some kind of SSO token (a cookie, a corporate token, etc) that could be used to obtain an OAuth2 Access Token. Obviously, it needs another artifact that must be able to determine if the SSO token is still valid.

To use this flow with Kong, it is needed to create an artifact, or custom OAuth proxy, that will sit between the client application and the OAuth2 endpoint. This artifact will receive the user id and the password of the resource owner. The artifact will validate also the credentials (probably using an LDAP server) and finally will interact with the OAuth2/token endpoint to get an OAuth2 access token that will be sent back to the client application. To make sure that only this artifact is able to obtain this access token, the provision_key will be used as a parameter to the OAuth2/token call.

The following diagram describes the flow:

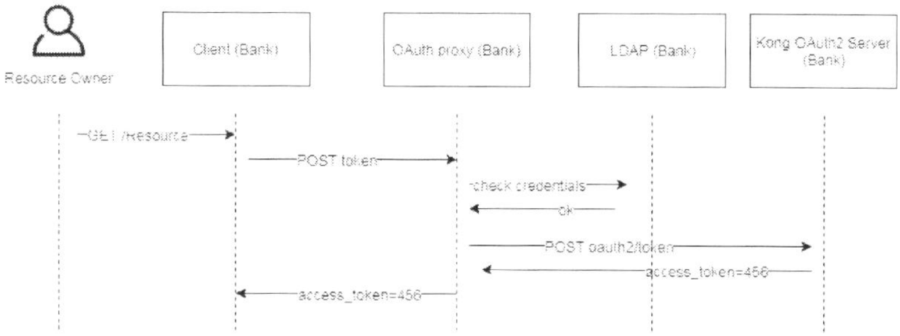

This curl instruction will be used to configure the Resource Owner Password Credentials flow:

```
$ curl -X POST http://localhost:8001/apis/movies/plugins \
    --data "name=oauth2" \
    --data "config.scopes=ratings,revenue" \
    --data "config.enable_password_grant=true"
```

As with the other grants, these steps must be done, as described in section "Enabling OAuth2 plugin":

- Create a Consumer (POST **http://localhost:8001/consumers/**)
- Create an Application (POST POST **http://localhost:8001/consumers/{consumer_id}/oauth2**).

To get an OAuth2 Access Token, the artifact between the client application and the OAuth2 endpoint will do this call:

```
$ curl -X POST https://localhost:8443/movies/oauth2/token \
    --data "client_id=fIeXHLeDwSuaCoHA0Bh2IgUeurBmX3Gt" \
    --data "client_secret=hhRrADE3XYjZp6DBU5ezRVpDt1gkkfK6" \
    --data "grant_type=password" \
    --data "provision_key=Nt1iqLe6CPN9Gv91L1nPDLlvzJgYZ5K2" \
    --data "scope=revenue" \
    --data "authenticated_userid=userid123"
```

The output of curl will be:

```
{
    "refresh_token": "1XwV5uuzdaX6InOM7otIxKKVklOmDy5F",
    "token_type": "bearer",
    "access_token": "oNMSjPVAVCmQVSQqt2jESOrQ2eHHWKRB",
    "expires_in": 7200
}
```

Sometimes it is needed to use the parameter -k in curl, in order to avoid SSL certification problems.

That access_token can be used to interact with the Movies API, passing the token in an Authorization header:

```
curl -X GET http://localhost:8000/movies \
  -H 'Authorization: Bearer oNMSjPVAVCmQVSQqt2jESOrQ2eHHWKRB'
```

If the Authorization header is missing, or the token is used after its expiration time, Kong will return an *HTTP 401 Unauthorized*.

Implicit grant

The Implicit grant is an OAuth2 flow very similar to the Authorization Code. This flow will typically be used by Single Page Applications (SPA) written in JavaScript that do not have the ability to safely store any secret. In that case, this flow is not returning a refresh_token, because the client application will not be able to store it.

Another main difference between the Implicit grant and the Authorization code grant is that in the Implicit grant, the Oauth2 endpoint is returning directly the access token in the redirection URL, and not a temporary code.

This is the less secure OAuth2 grant, so only very short-lived access tokens should be issued.

Refresh Token grant

The typical OAuth2 access token will have an expiration time of around 5 minutes (300 seconds). If a client application uses an expired access token, Kong will return an *HTTP 401 Unauthorized* with this response:

```
{
    "error_description": "The access token is invalid or has
expired",
    "error": "invalid_token"
}
```

In order to obtain a new access token, a possibility could be to request that the resource owners provide their credentials again. Obviously, once resource owners grant a third-party access to their personal data, they expect the client applications to use that information autonomously, not having to be asked for their credentials again and again.

OAuth2 provides an additional grant, or Refresh Token, that can be used to request new access tokens on behalf of the user. The endpoint that will be used to generate a new access token will be oauth2/token and it will use these parameters:

- grant_type - It must be: refresh_token
- client_id - The client ID associated with this Consumer and Application
- client_secret - The client secret associated with this Consumer and Application
- refresh_token - It must contain a previously issued refresh token

This sample curl shows how to get a refresh token:

```
$ curl -X POST https://localhost:8443/movies/oauth2/token \
    --data "grant_type=refresh_token" \
    --data "client_id=fIeXHLeDwSuaCoHA0Bh2IgUeurBmX3Gt" \
    --data "client_secret=hhRrADE3XYjZp6DBU5ezRVpDt1gkkfK6" \
    --data "refresh_token=1XwV5uuzdaX6InOM7otIxKKVklOmDy5F"
```

Upon completion, the OAuth2 server would return a JSON object like this:

```
{
    "refresh_token": "5WrRlyTeYh7V2ELWQTtbpG6cUEAoRL8e",
    "token_type": "bearer",
    "access_token": "CpeACPZLMhUiMK5tOA9Xcy22Qn1qitHS",
```

```
    "expires_in": 7200
}
```

The new refresh token will be different from the previous one. If the client application tries to invoke the grant passing a refresh token that was used previously, Kong will return an *HTTP 400 Bad Request* with this error:

```
{
    "error_description": "Invalid refresh_token",
    "error": "invalid_request"
}
```

OpenID Connect

As described in the previous section, OAuth2 is an authorization framework that can be very useful for resource owners to grant temporary access to their personal information and to perform operations on their behalf. However, OAuth2 does not provide any facility to identify the end-user who has granted the permissions, because OAuth2 is not intended to be used to provide identity information.

OpenID Connect was born in 2014 as an identity layer on top of OAuth2. Unlike OAuth2, OpenID Connect provides to client applications a mechanism to identify to the resource owners who has granted permissions.

OpenID Connect has gained traction due to the release of the UK Open Banking APIs. These APIs are based on OAuth2, but the specification explicitly mandates the use of OpenID Connect on top of OAuth2 to be able to add identity information.

New and modified flows

This table summarizes the flows that OpenID Connect has modified or added on top of OAuth2:

Flow	New or Modified	Description
Authorization Code	Modified	In OpenID Connect, the scope must contain the value *openid* although other scopes may be present. The response of the /token endpoint will include an

Flow	New or Modified	Description
		additional field (id_token) that contains a JWT with identity information.
Implicit Flow	Modified	The scope must contain the value *openid* although other scopes may be present. The response of the /authorize endpoint will include an additional field (id_token) that contains a JWT with identity information.
Hybrid Flow	New	This flow is designed to provide flexibility; some of the tokens are returned in the /token endpoint or in the /authorize. The response of the /authorize endpoint depends on the value of the parameter response_type, which can be one of these three choices: 1) code id_token ; 2) code token ; 3) code id_token token.

The ID Token

The ID Token is a JSON Web Token (JWT) that contains a set of claims with identity information. The standard claims are:

Claim	Type
sub	string
name	string
given_name	string
family_name	string
middle_name	string
nickname	string
preferred_username	string
profile	string
picture	string
website	string
email	string
email_verified	boolean

Claim	Type
gender	string
birthdate	string
zoneinfo	string
locale	string
phone_number	string
phone_number_verified	boolean
address	JSON object
updated_at	number

New endpoints

OpenID Connect introduces a new endpoint: /userinfo. This new endpoint can be used either with GET or with POST and accepts an Authorization header that must contain an OAuth2 Access Token. The output of the endpoint will be a JSON object containing identity information of the resource owner. The fields of that JSON object will have the same names shown in the list of standard claims of the previous section.

Kong support for OpenID Connect

Although Kong Community Edition does not include yet support for OpenID Connect, Kong Enterprise Edition includes a suite of plugins to support OpenID Connect. The plugins included in the suite are:

- OpenID Connect Verification Plugin
- OpenID Connect Authentication Plugin
- OpenID Connect Protection Plugin
- OpenID Connect Revocation Plugin
- OpenID Connect Dereferencing Plugin

Protecting APIs with JWT

OAuth2 and OpenID Connect are the most common authorization and authentication frameworks that are used today to protect APIs. However, in some scenarios, it may make sense to use JSON Web Tokens (JWT - pronounced: “jot”) as an alternate way to protect an API. For example:

- Usually, after an OAuth2 flow, it is common to generate a JWT to interact with microservices. If one of those microservices tries to invoke to another API, it may be interesting to directly use the same JWT that was used to interact with the microservice.
- To secure mobile applications. There are some scenarios in which a mobile application could use JWT as an authorization token to interact with an API.

Kong supports out-of-the-box the validation of JWT tokens. Unfortunately, it does not yet support the generation of JWT; in case that functionality is needed in a project, it may be necessary to write a custom Kong plugin.

What is a JSON Web Token?

JSON Web Tokens (JWT) are defined in the RFC 7519. It is basically a compact and self-contained way to carry a set of claims between two parts. A JWT is composed of three Base64 strings separated by dots:

```
eyJhbGciOiJIUzI1NiIsInR5cCI6IkpXVCJ9.eyJzdWIiOiIxMjMiLCJuYW1
lIjoiSm9hbyBNYXJ0aW5zIn0.TfesTf-QPpJu2y01B6rwQfKuiQTDza32Y3
QPXWcx7Nk
```

The three strings are:

- A Header. It is a JSON object that usually contains two attributes: 1) A hash algorithm (HS256, RS256, etc); 2) A type: JWT.
- A Payload. It is a JSON containing a set of attributes or claims like: iss (Issuer) sub (Subject) exp (Expiration) aud (Audience) etc.
- A signature.

When an API Gateway or a microservice is invoked using a JWT included in an Authorization header, it will be necessary to perform the following validations:

- Check if the JWT has not expired
- Check if the audience is the adequate
- Check if the JWT was signed by a known party (usually another API Gateway)

Enabling the JWT plugin

The following instruction will enable the JWT plugin in the Movies API. The plugin will verify as well that the JWT has not expired yet. The plugin will be configured to use the claim 'iss' to identify the key that will be used to validate the token:

```
$ curl -X POST http://localhost:8001/apis/movies/plugins \
    --data "name=jwt" \
    --data "config.claims_to_verify=exp"
```

Upon completion of that instruction, any invocation to the Movies API will return an *HTTP 401 Unauthorized*, unless a valid JWT is passed in an Authorization header and at least a Consumer has been configured with a key that can be used to validate that token.

Adding JWT credentials to a Consumer

Before trying to use the Movies API with a JWT, it is necessary to associate with an existing Consumer a credential that will be used to validate the JWT.

Kong supports different algorithms to validate JWT:

- HS256 (the default)
- RS256
- ES256

The following instruction creates an HS256 credential for a Consumer named PurpleMall:

```
$ curl -X POST http://localhost:8001/consumers/PurpleMall/
jwt \
    --header "Content-Type: application/x-www-form-
urlencoded"
```

The output of that command will be:

```
{
    "created_at":1517350724000,
    "id":"2ea7c77c-a627-4917-ada6-1bb052a46e03",
    "algorithm":"HS256",
    "key":"gn0DactcwAMKUmA0iuPVXkBnVjxxIbVW",
    "secret":"Rz3fBOsIWvdoT3SAf1LLc2xIUkLEE1iC",
```

```
    "consumer_id":"d25a7eaf-c44b-4425-97c5-4683f989b355"
}
```

The most important attributes of that output are:

- Key - Identifies the credential. That value must be included in the 'iss' claim of the JWT in order to be able to identify the credentials to be used to validate the JWT
- Secret - It is the secret used in the HS256 algorithm to calculate the signature.

Putting it all together

Once the API and the Consumer have been properly configured, the next step is to create a valid JWT for testing purposes. There are many online JWT generators available. A simple search on Google would provide different useful websites that provide the ability to generate and validate JWT. Probably the best known is JWT.IO, a simple website that provides a useful interface to validate and to generate JWT.

The steps required to generate a JWT are:

Step	**Description**
Navigate with your browser to **https://jwt.io/**	A page with a sample JWT will appear. The JWT will be shown on the left side as Encoded, and in the right side as Decoded.
Maintain the Header as it is.	Maintain the algorithm to be HS256.
Add a "iss" claim in the payload	The value should be the same than the "key" property associated with the JWT credential in the Consumer
Add a "exp" claim in the payload	The value should be the current time (in seconds) plus 60 or 90 seconds
Type the secret in the signature	The value should be the same than the "secret" property associated with the JWT credential in the Consumer
Copy the Encoded JWT to the clipboard	It should contain the claims and a signature based on the secret.

This is a sample of the header and payload:

```
{
  "alg": "HS256",
  "typ": "JWT"
}
{
  "sub": "1234",
  "name": "Simon Warren",
  "iss" : "gn0DactcwAMKUmA0iuPVXkBnVjxxIbVW",
  "exp" : 1517951758
}
```

This is a sample of that JWT, but encoded (secret: Rz3fBOslWv-doT3SAf1LLc2xlUkLEE1iC):

```
eyJhbGciOiJIUzI1NiIsInR5cCI6IkpXVCJ9.eyJzdWIiOiIxMjM0Iiwi
bmFtZSI6IlNpbW9uIFdhcnJlbiIsImlzcyI6ImduMERhY3RjdOFNS1VtQ
TBpdVBWWGtCblZqeHhJYlZXIiwiZXhwIjoxNTE3OTUxNzU4fQ.s9nHjy6
knQMllCSN-Fqd9q165-pQwjBhi2bueTE-UzM
```

To interact with the Movies API, the JWT must be included in an Authorization header:

```
$ curl -X GET http://localhost:8000/movies \
   --header "Authorization: Bearer
eyJhbGciOiJIUzI1NiIsInR5cCI6IkpXVCJ9.eyJzdWIiOiIxMjM0Iiwi
bmFtZSI6IlNpbW9uIFdhcnJlbiIsImlzcyI6ImduMERhY3RjdOFNS1VtQ
TBpdVBWWGtCblZqeHhJYlZXIiwiZXhwIjoxNTE3OTUxNzU4fQ.s9nHjy6
knQMllCSN-Fqd9q165-pQwjBhi2bueTE-UzM"
```

If the JWT was signed properly, the API would return an *HTTP 200* with the response. In case the token JWT has expired, Kong will return an *HTTP 401 Unauthorized* with a message explaining that the JWT expired. In case the claim "iss" contains a value different than the key associated with the Consumer, Kong would return an *HTTP 403 Forbidden*, with a message saying that no credentials were found for that given 'iss'.

CORS

Cross-Origin Resource Sharing (CORS) is a W3C Recommendation that allows browsers to interact with resources that are available on domains outside the domain from which the page was downloaded. Although it is common in a web page to include images and style sheets of other domains, any modern browser will protect the execution of JavaScript that tries to interact with APIs belonging to other domains.

CORS is based on response headers. Basically, when CORS is enabled in a particular API served from an API Gateway, a response header called Access-Control-Allow-Origin will be added to the response.

That header can be configured with different values. Some examples assuming that CORS is enabled in an API Gateway in the domain a.com:

- Access-Control-Allow-Origin: **http://b.com**. With this configuration, any web page found in b.com will be able to interact with APIs found in a.com. However, if a web page found in c.com tries to interact with this gateway, the browser would block it.
- Access-Control-Allow-Origin: * . With this configuration, the APIs of a.com will be available to any application running on any domain.

To use CORS in Kong, it is enough to enable the plugin on any API, for example in Movies:

```
curl -X POST http://localhost:8001/apis/movies/plugins/ \
  --header 'content-type: application/x-www-form-urlencoded'
\
  --data "name=cors"
```

The output of curl will be:

```
{
    "created_at":1517354766000,
    "config":
    {
        "credentials":false,
        "preflight_continue":false
    },
    "id":"4e9f2a99-dee0-4c3d-a193-46a8f6ff0fab",
    "name":"cors",
    "api_id":"bd5baf99-7838-46b7-a81f-575a3726c7b5",
    "enabled":true
}
```

Any call to a Movies API will now include these headers. From now on, a new header (Access-Control-Allow-Origin) will be included in the response:

```
HTTP/1.1 200 OK
Content-Type: application/json; charset=utf-8
Content-Length: 622
Connection: keep-alive
X-Powered-By: Express
X-Content-Type-Options: nosniff
```

```
ETag: W/"26e-4lY2V90zz3jPaMtUYoDpyO0zGQw"
Date: Tue, 30 Jan 2018 23:28:13 GMT
Access-Control-Allow-Origin: *
X-Kong-Upstream-Latency: 2
X-Kong-Proxy-Latency: 1
Via: kong/0.11.2
```

Conclusion

API Security is a complex topic, since APIs can be protected with a variety of choices, including keys, OAuth, OpenID Connect, JWT, and CORS. Kong Gateway includes out-of-the-box different plugins that can be used to create a robust security architecture.

You have now reached the end of this book. We hope you have learned everything you need to take advantage of Kong.

11136592R00111

Printed in Germany
by Amazon Distribution
GmbH, Leipzig